CIVIL WAR BATTLEFIELDS THEN & NOW

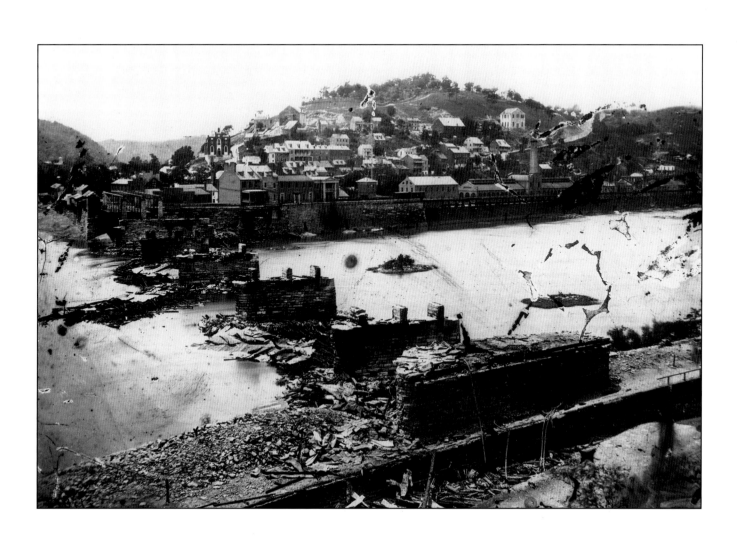

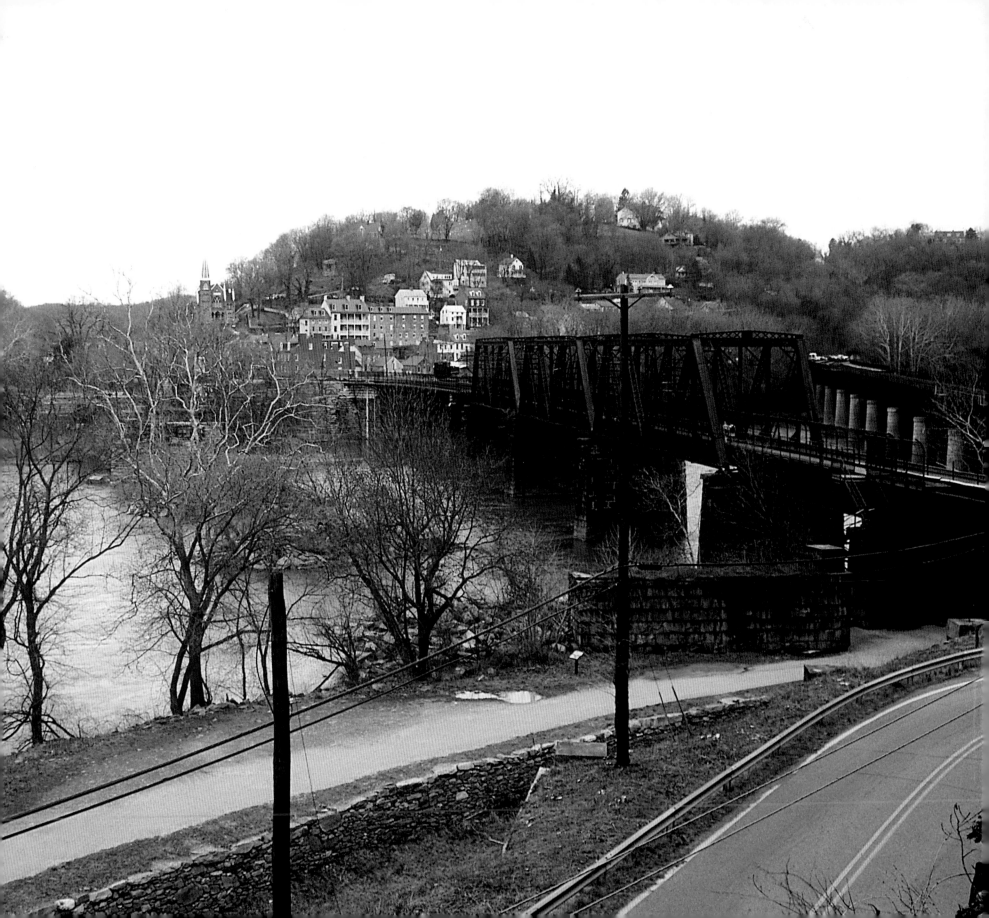

CIVIL WAR BATTLEFIELDS THEN & NOW

JAMES CAMPI, JR.

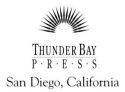

THUNDER BAY
P·R·E·S·S

San Diego, California

Thunder Bay Press
An imprint of the Advantage Publishers Group
5880 Oberlin Drive, San Diego, CA 92121-4794
www.thunderbaybooks.com

Produced by PRC Publishing Ltd,
64 Brewery Road, London N7 9NT, England

A member of **Chrysalis** Books plc

All notations of errors or omissions should be addressed to Thunder Bay Press,
editorial department, at the above address. All other correspondence (author inquiries,
permissions, and rights) concerning the content of this book should be addressed to
PRC Publishing Ltd, 64 Brewery Road, London N7 9NT, England.

ISBN 1-57145-865-4

Library of Congress Cataloging-in-Publication Data available upon request.

Printed in Taiwan

1 2 3 4 5 06 05 04 03 02

To my parents, James and Claire.

Author's note

The photographs in this book are presented chronologically in order to tell the larger story of the struggle between the states. Except in rare instances, all of the period photographs were taken during the war or in its immediate aftermath. However, because many of the battlefields of the Civil War—particularly those in the Western theater—were not photographed until many years after the end of the conflict, unavoidable gaps exist. In addition, several of the images were taken a year or more after the battles they describe. For example, the photographs of the Stone House and Sudley Church were taken nearly a year after the First Battle of Manassas, after the Confederates evacuated the area. Maps have been included where possible for the reader's ease of reference, but this has not been possible in every case. All the maps that appear in this book are supplied courtesy of the National Park Service.

Acknowledgments

This book would not have been possible without the yeoman's work done by historians of Civil War photography in the past few decades. They have taken upon themselves the monumental task of sifting through old stereoviews and glass plates to document the visual record of the war. In particular, I am indebted to William A. Frassanito, whose books on Civil War photography—*Gettysburg, A Journey in Time*; *Antietam, The Photographic Legacy of America's Bloodiest Day*; *Grant and Lee, The Virginia Campaigns 1864–1865*; and *Early Photography at Gettysburg*—have created an entire generation of buffs who scour Civil War battlefields looking for the exact spot where wartime photographs were taken. I also referred to William C. Davis's six-volume study, *Embattled Confederacy: The Image of War, 1861–1865*, originally published by the National Historical Society and a masterpiece of Civil War history and photography. Finally, I would be remiss if I failed to mention the recently published *Charleston at War* by Jack Thomson, whose walking tours of Charleston are a necessity for any student of the war.

In addition, I want to thank the photographers who contributed to the contemporary images in this book: My good friend Shawn McBurney, who I first met on the Fredericksburg battlefield nearly ten years ago; Robert Price, whose commitment to Civil War battlefield preservation is equaled by his talent behind the lens; and Alexander Mitchell, the author of *Washington Then and Now*, who braved briars and mountains to get the correct shot each time. I also want to thank Martin Howard and Louise Daubeny of Chrysalis Books, who patiently worked with me to select the photographs and write the text of the book. Finally, I want to thank my wife, Jennifer, for indulging my interest in the war and helping proofread and edit this book.

Credits

INTRODUCTION

More than 140 years have passed since Confederate guns first fired on Fort Sumter. The resulting two-day artillery duel over possession of a small masonry fort in Charleston Harbor signaled the beginning of the Civil War, the greatest conflict in U.S. history. For four long years, North and South would clash in 10,000 battles and skirmishes that defined America as a nation. More than 625,000 soldiers and 50,000 civilians perished as a result.

Seven generations later, the Civil War continues to capture the imagination of Americans for many reasons. The war is often referred to as the last old-fashioned war and first modern war, and certainly the struggle contained elements of both. Because of the enormous number of men enrolled in the Union and Confederate armies, millions of today's Americans can trace their ancestry back to the war. And, unlike earlier conflicts, so many of the men in blue and gray were prolific writers that thousands of eyewitness accounts of the war survive as an invaluable resource for historians.

However, it is the photography of the Civil War that most often fascinates enthusiasts of the war today. Photography made the Civil War the first conflict in which noncombatants far from the battlefield could see for themselves the misery and carnage of war. Obscure landmarks such as the Stone House at Manassas and Devil's Den at Gettysburg were reproduced as newspaper woodcuts and brought to life at popular photography exhibitions.

For the first time as well, civilians had an opportunity to view haunting photographs of the battlefield dead. Unlike the practice in previous conflicts, these stark images were neither romanticized nor glorified by a painter's brush. Referring to the photographs of the dead at Antietam, an unknown *New York Times* reporter wrote, "Mr. Brady has done something to bring to us the terrible reality and earnestness of the war. If he has not brought bodies and laid them in our door-yards and among our streets, he has done something very like it." These photographs of the human wreckage of war jolted the public consciousness in a manner similar to that of the television images of the Vietnam War a century later.

When the Civil War began, photography was still in its infancy and consisted mostly of portraiture. America's most celebrated photographer at the time, Mathew Brady, was renowned for the large "imperial" portraits that hung in his comfortable New York and Washington galleries. With the coming of war, Brady switched gears and focused much of his attention on images taken from "the seat of war." His photography teams followed the armies through four years of conflict. When in the field, Brady often placed himself in the camera's view, and his pointed beard and pince-nez glasses are familiar sights in his wartime views. Ironically, the war that made Brady a legend left him penniless and led to the closure of his once-famous galleries.

Despite the omnipresence of the Brady name on Civil War–era photographs, Brady rarely if ever took any battlefield photographs. Instead he left that to his talented assistants, the most prominent of whom were Alexander Gardner, the manager of Brady's Washington gallery, and James F. Gibson. It was this pair, rather than Brady, who would take the images of the dead at Antietam. Later, the two were joined by another photographer, Timothy O'Sullivan, to take a series of equally dramatic photos at Gettysburg. By that time, Gardner had parted with Brady and set up his own gallery in Washington.

In addition to these gentlemen, several other photographers would earn their reputations during the war. Captain Andrew Russell was assigned by Union General Herman Haupt to document the engineering innovations of the Union army, as well as to photograph the battlefields of the war. George N. Barnard, another Brady associate, became the official photographer of the Union armies in the Western theater. Many of Barnard's photos of General William T. Sherman's campaign through Georgia and the Carolinas appear in the latter pages of this book.

The Confederates boasted several wartime photographers as well, although the scarcity of materials for both making and reproducing photographs in the blockade-starved South hampered their efforts. One of the first images of the war, showing the Stars and Bars of the Confederacy flying proudly over Fort Sumter, was taken by F. K. Houston of Charleston. Arguably the best-known Confederate photographer was another Charlestonian, George S. Cook, whose image of a Union shell bursting inside battered Sumter is one of the most noteworthy of the war.

These early pioneers in the profession of war photography were able to invoke powerful emotions with their images of the people, places, and events of the Civil War. In fact, so powerful were the photographs that, in the years immediately following the war, Americans tried to put both the war and its photographs behind them. The images, and the memories they conjured up, were simply too painful. Many of the images and original glass plates were lost, some winding up as glass for greenhouses. Fortunately, in the decades after the war, the federal government realized the enormous historical significance of the photos. They purchased the bankrupt Brady's remaining photos for $25,000 and began accumulating other wartime images as well. In addition, other historically minded organizations, such as the Massachusetts Commandery of the Military Order of the Loyal Legion, amassed large collections of Civil War period photographs. Today, many of these images are preserved at the Library of Congress, the National Archives, and the U.S. Army Military Institute in Carlisle, Pennsylvania, where they will remain to captivate and fascinate future generations.

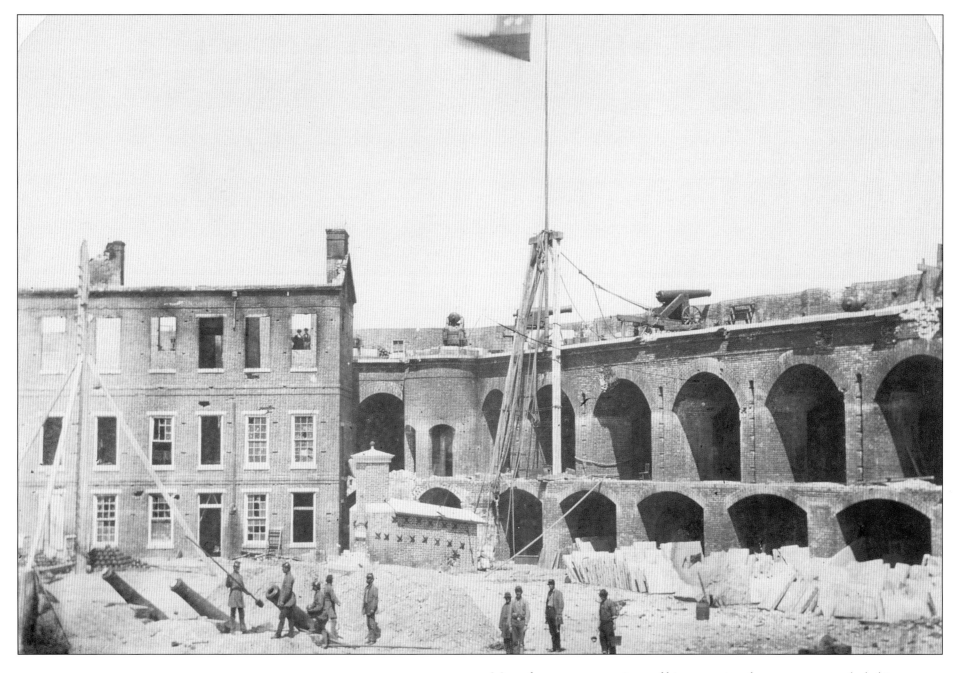

More than two generations of bitter sectional controversy exploded into armed conflict on April 12, 1861, when Confederate guns fired on Fort Sumter. Ironically, no one was killed during the bombardment. Only after the guns fell silent were two Union soldiers injured firing a salute, making them the first casualties of America's bloodiest war. A few hours later, the Stars and Bars of the Confederate States were unfurled over Sumter.

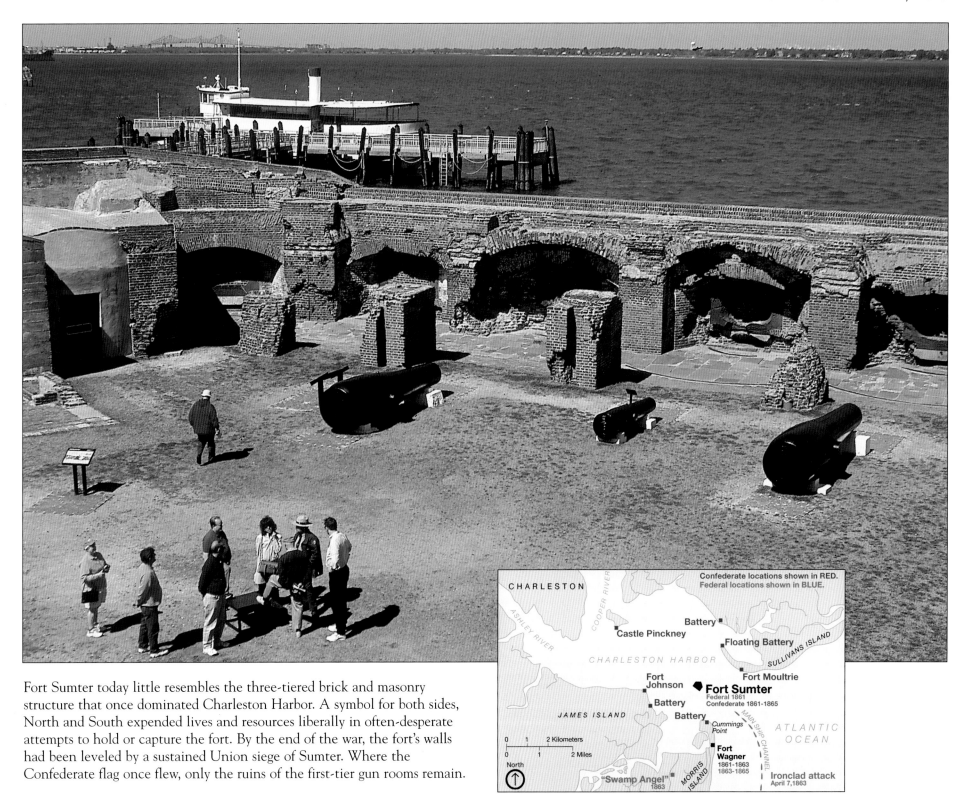

Fort Sumter today little resembles the three-tiered brick and masonry structure that once dominated Charleston Harbor. A symbol for both sides, North and South expended lives and resources liberally in often-desperate attempts to hold or capture the fort. By the end of the war, the fort's walls had been leveled by a sustained Union siege of Sumter. Where the Confederate flag once flew, only the ruins of the first-tier gun rooms remain.

Confederate locations shown in RED.
Federal locations shown in BLUE.

CHARLESTON

ASHLEY RIVER

COOPER RIVER

Castle Pinckney

Battery

Floating Battery

SULLIVANS ISLAND

CHARLESTON HARBOR

Fort Moultrie

Fort Johnson

Fort Sumter
Federal 1861
Confederate 1861-1865

Battery

JAMES ISLAND

Battery

Cummings Point

MAIN SHIP CHANNEL

ATLANTIC OCEAN

Fort Wagner
1861-1863
1863-1865

Ironclad attack
April 7, 1863

0 1 2 Kilometers
0 1 2 Miles

North

"Swamp Angel" 1863

MORRIS ISLAND

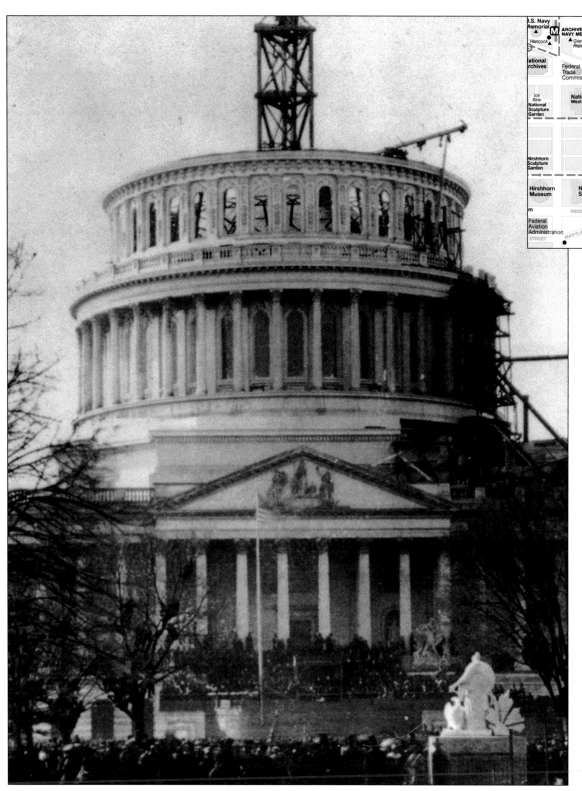

After the surrender of Fort Sumter, the nation's attention turned to the respective capitals of the two nations. Washington, D.C., became a city under siege, and a Confederate flag on Arlington Heights was visible from the White House. Southerners quickly erected batteries along the Potomac, effectively blockading the city. In response, government buildings were barricaded and turned into barracks, and Union troops were quartered in the Capitol Rotunda, beneath its unfinished dome.

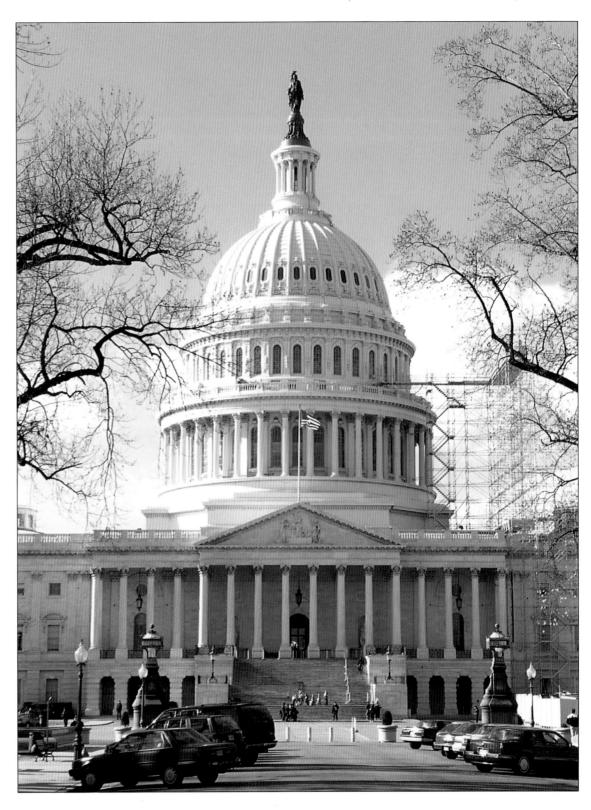

In the early days of the war, there was some discussion about discontinuing the renovation of the U.S. Capitol and its enormous new dome. The new president, Abraham Lincoln, would have none of this defeatist talk. He ordered the construction work to continue, as a "symbol that the Union would go on." Four years later, in March 1865, Lincoln would be inaugurated to a second term beneath a completed dome.

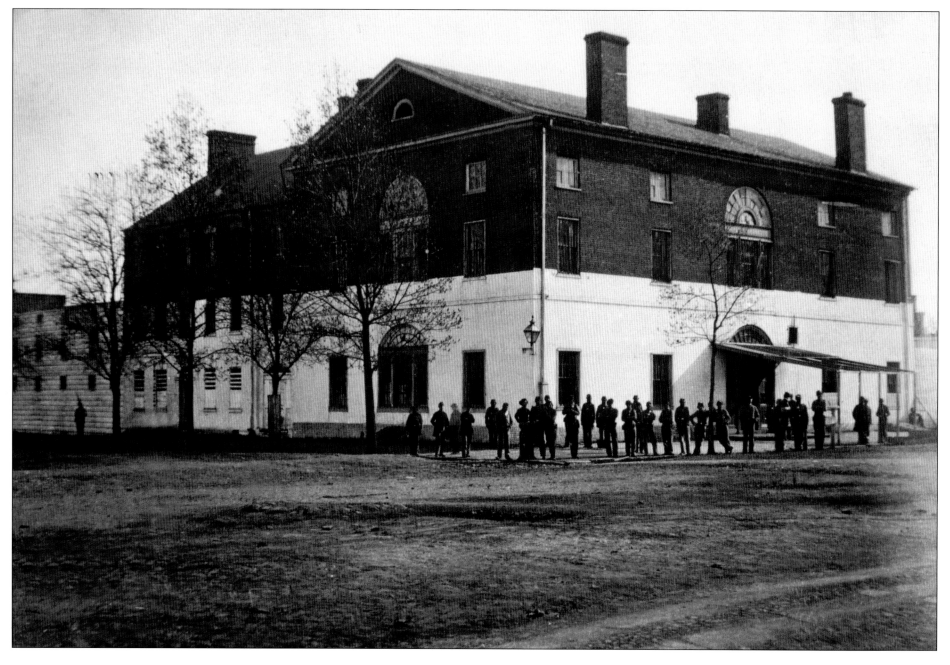

Prior to the war, Washington was considered a Southern city, with slavery permitted within its limits. As a result, the Union capital was crawling with Confederate sympathizers, many longing for the day when their compatriots across the river would force the Lincoln Administration to flee. Many of these sympathizers did more than just long for liberation; several turned to spying as a method of ensuring the defeat of the Northerners in their midst.

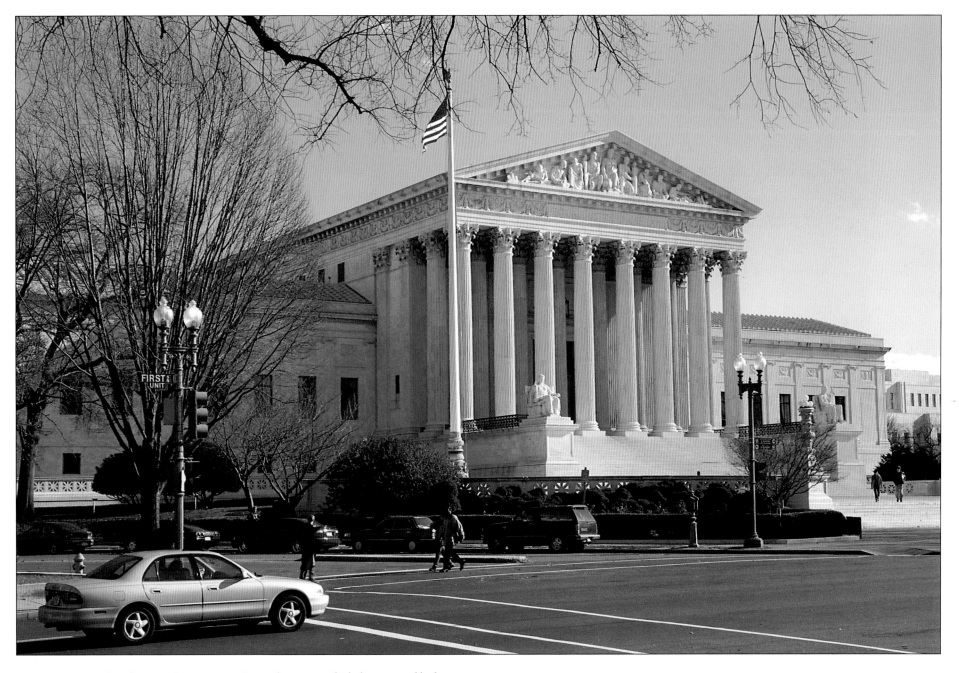

In response to the threat of espionage, Lincoln suspended the writ of habeas corpus and threw several suspected Rebel spies into the Old Capitol Prison, located on the present site of the U.S. Supreme Court. Among the notables incarcerated within the prison's walls was Rose O'Neill Greenhow, the spy who would warn the Confederate army of the Union march on Manassas. Her warning enabled the Southern army to concentrate its forces south of Bull Run.

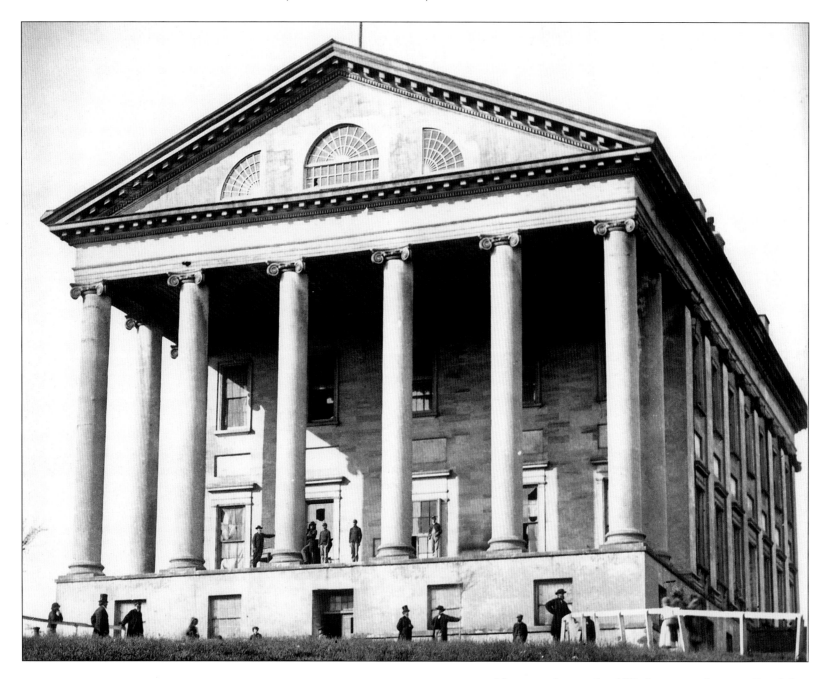

Ninety miles south of Washington, the new Confederate government was establishing itself in the manufacturing center of Richmond, Virginia. Representatives from thirteen Southern states gathered in the stately Virginia Capitol, designed by Thomas Jefferson in 1788. As the war dragged on, the Capitol would be the scene of rancorous debates over the handling of the war, the first conscription in America, and the enlistment of slaves in the war's waning days.

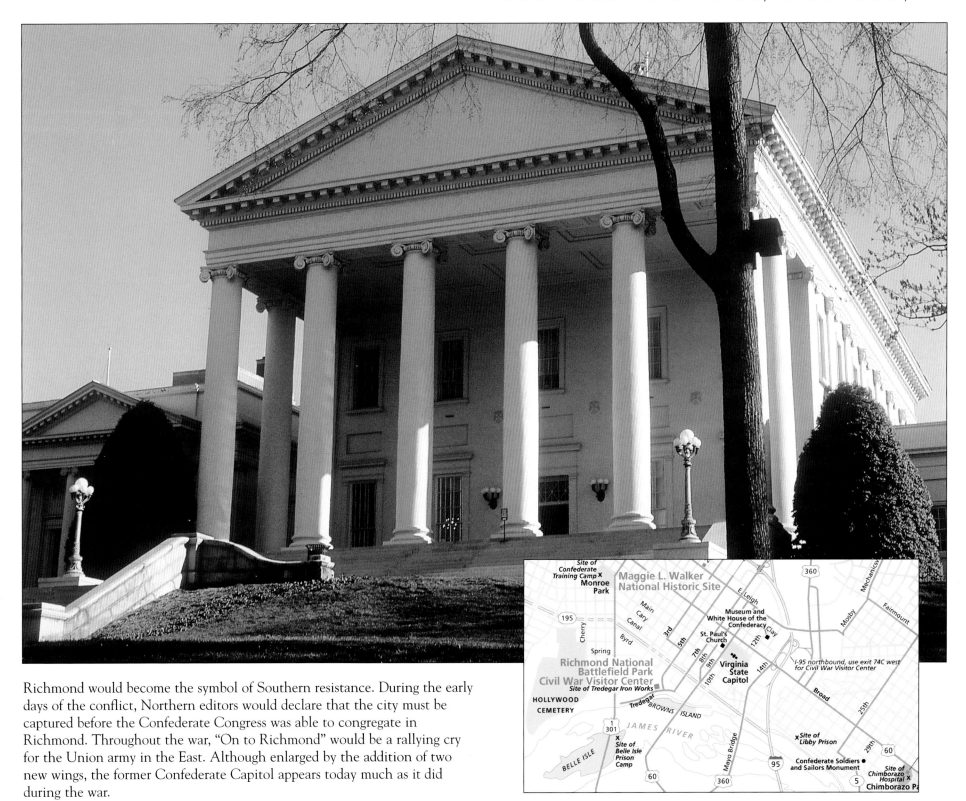

Richmond would become the symbol of Southern resistance. During the early days of the conflict, Northern editors would declare that the city must be captured before the Confederate Congress was able to congregate in Richmond. Throughout the war, "On to Richmond" would be a rallying cry for the Union army in the East. Although enlarged by the addition of two new wings, the former Confederate Capitol appears today much as it did during the war.

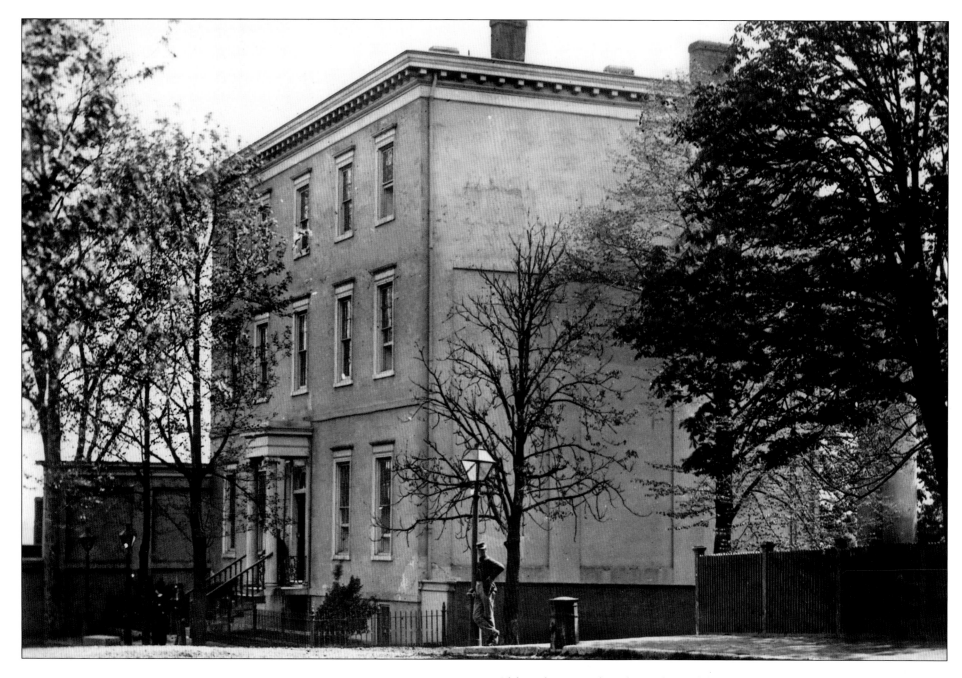

Although gray rather than white, the Confederate executive mansion is referred to as the "White House of the Confederacy." Within these walls, the proud and often difficult Jefferson Davis would preside over the Southern experiment in nationhood. Davis would often meet with his cabinet and generals in this three-story building. It was here that Davis met with his most successful commander, Robert E. Lee, to plan the ill-fated Gettysburg campaign.

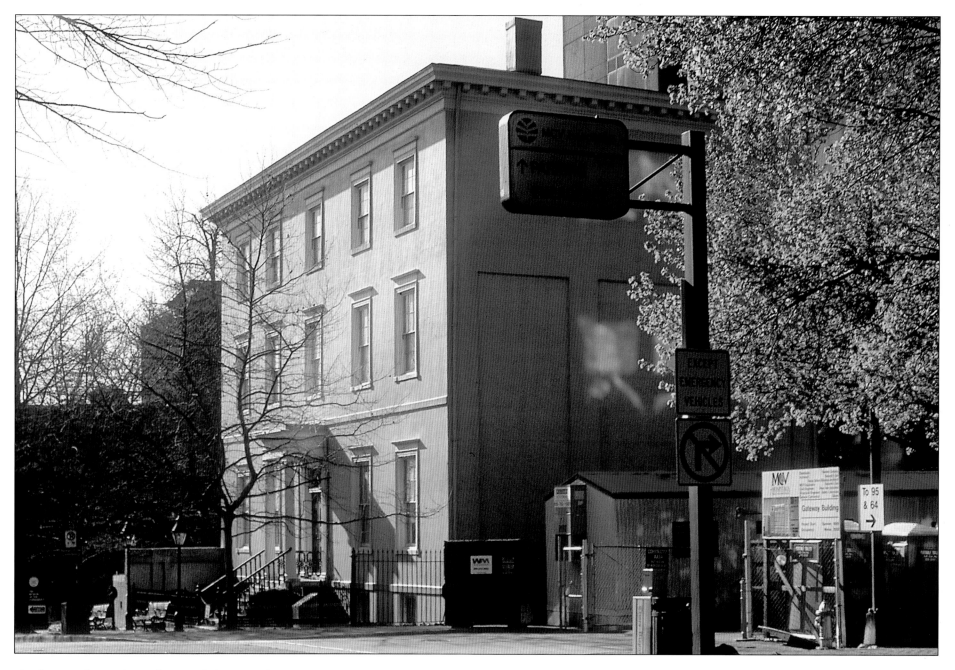

As the war dragged on, the Confederate White House became something of a refuge for President Davis from the bitter denunciations of his many critics. When the city was evacuated in 1865, the house would serve as Union army headquarters, and President Abraham Lincoln would briefly sit at Davis's desk. Today the house has been restored to its wartime appearance and is located adjacent to the Museum of the Confederacy.

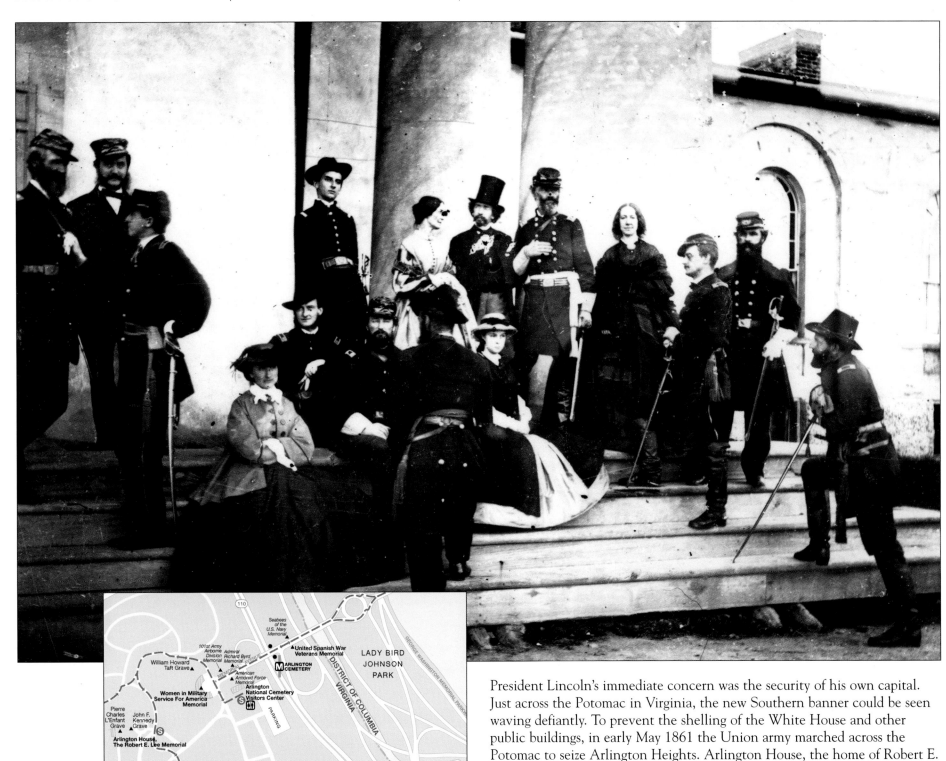

President Lincoln's immediate concern was the security of his own capital. Just across the Potomac in Virginia, the new Southern banner could be seen waving defiantly. To prevent the shelling of the White House and other public buildings, in early May 1861 the Union army marched across the Potomac to seize Arlington Heights. Arlington House, the home of Robert E. Lee, was occupied and served as a Northern army headquarters.

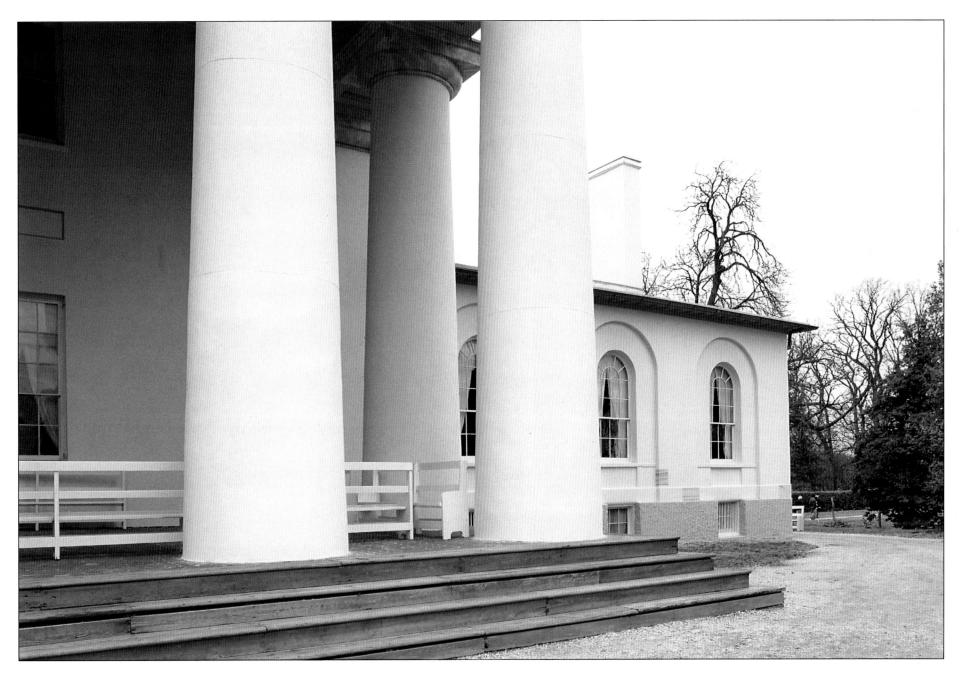

Arlington House, begun in 1802, would not be left unscathed by the Union occupation. Lee's wife was the daughter of Washington's step-grandson and only heir, and the house contained many Washington heirlooms that were eventually claimed by the federal government. By 1864, the Union Quartermaster General chose the Arlington House property as the location of a cemetery for war dead. Today, more than 245,000 American servicemen and their families are buried there.

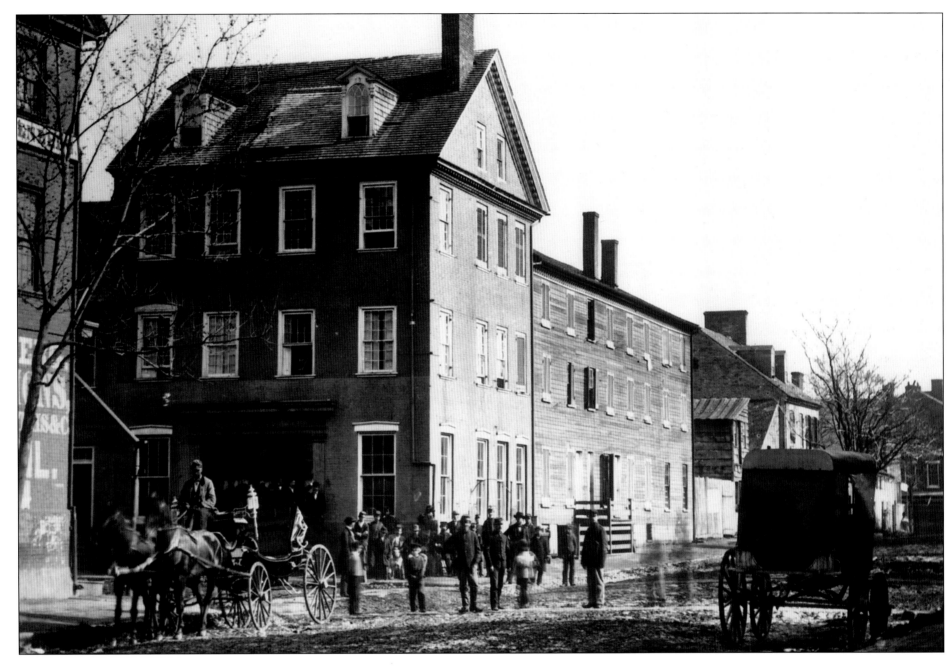

Although the Northern forces sent across the Potomac did not encounter any Confederate forces, the Union occupation of Arlington Heights and nearby Alexandria was not entirely bloodless. As Union Colonel Elmer Ellsworth rode into Alexandria at the head of his 11th New York Fire Zouave Regiment, he spotted the Rebel colors flying from the Marshall House, a local hotel. Ellsworth marched into the hotel, determined to make the banner his first war trophy.

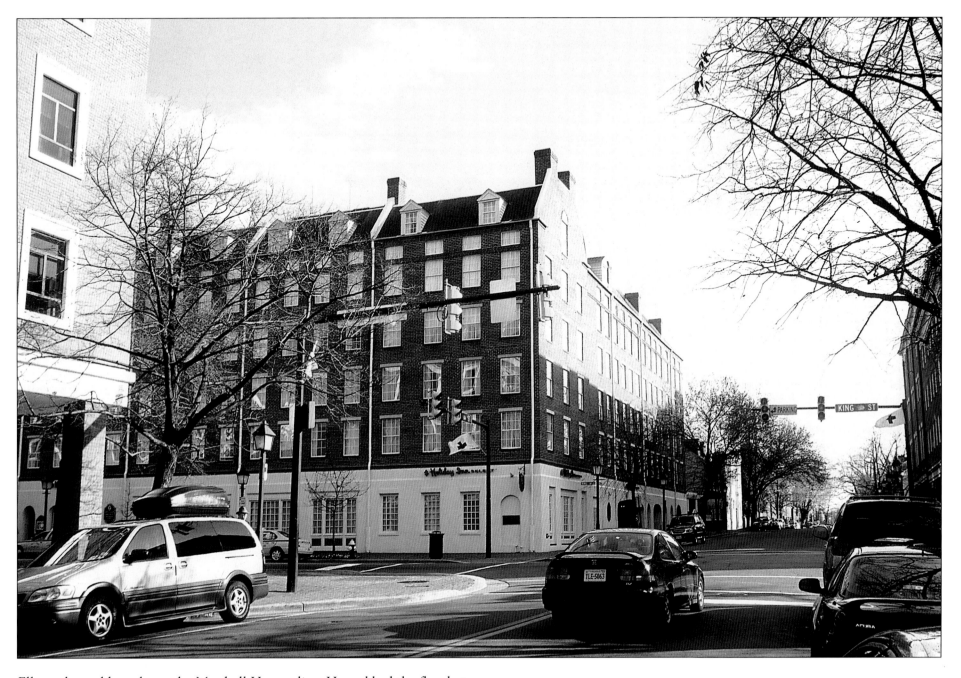

Ellsworth would not leave the Marshall House alive. He grabbed the flag, but as he walked down the steps, he was shot dead by the hotel's proprietor, who was in turn killed by one of Ellsworth's officers. As the North's first martyr, Ellsworth's body would lie in state in the White House. His men threatened to burn down the Marshall House, but the hotel would survive the war. Today a Holiday Inn stands on the site.

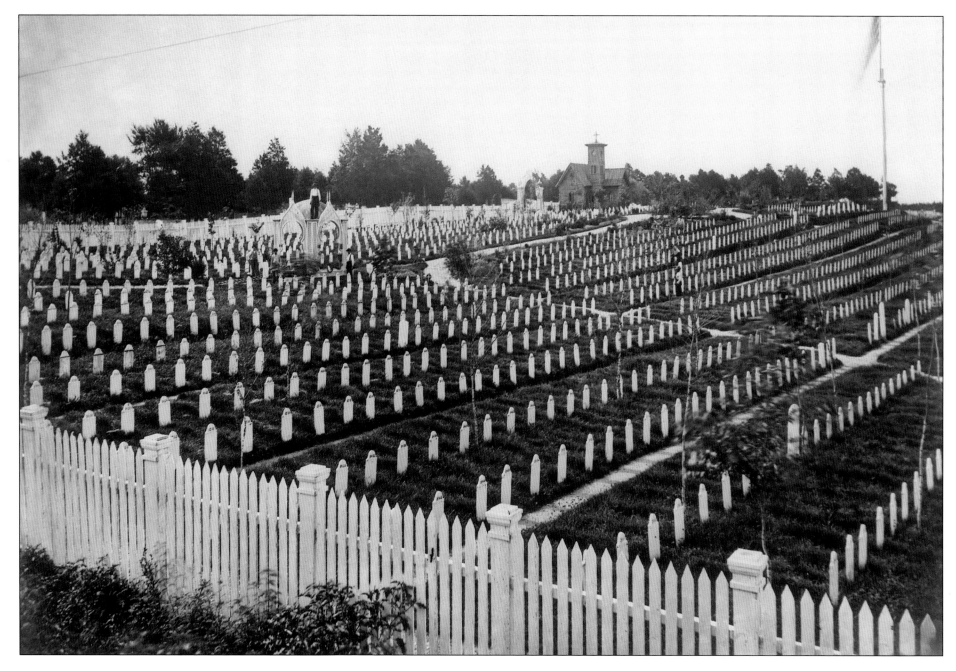

Occupied Alexandria would become the hub for Union operations in the East. The city was the terminus of the Orange and Alexandria Railroad, which snaked through northern and central Virginia. The railroad would become one of the principal supply lines of the Union, transporting men and munitions southward, and the sick and wounded back to the city's crowded hospitals. Far too many wound up buried in the rapidly expanding Alexandria National Cemetery.

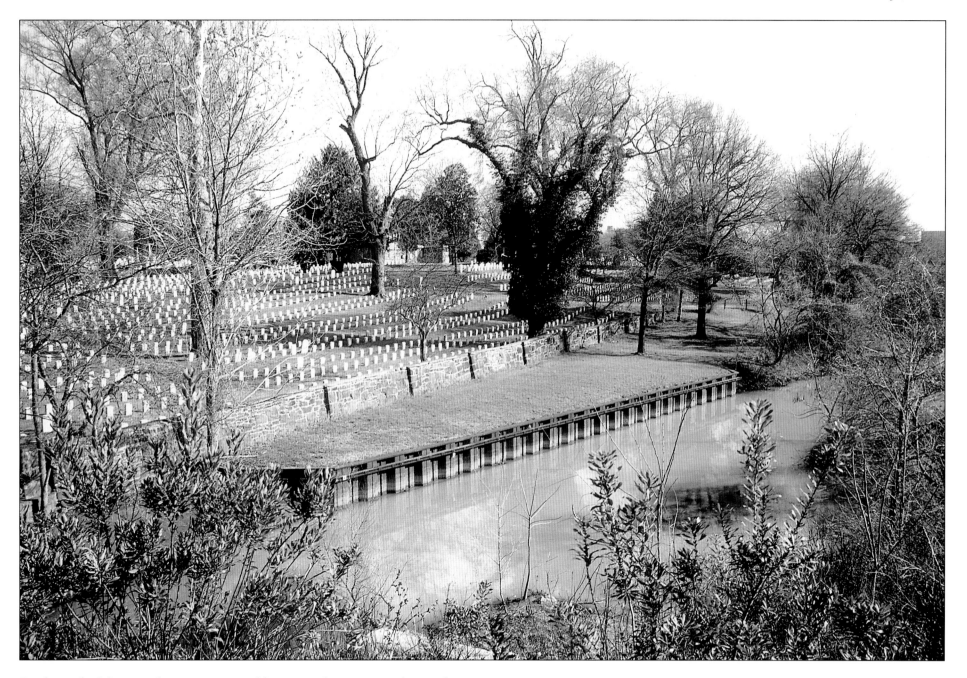

By the end of the war, the cemetery would contain the remains of more than 3,500 Union soldiers. Among those buried there are Joseph Squires, a Wisconsin native mortally wounded at Petersburg in 1864, and Joseph Wiggin, who spent his final hours in the Fairfax Seminary Hospital. Today the cemetery is nestled behind several other city cemeteries. The railroad bridge that carried the wounded back to Alexandria can still be seen nearby.

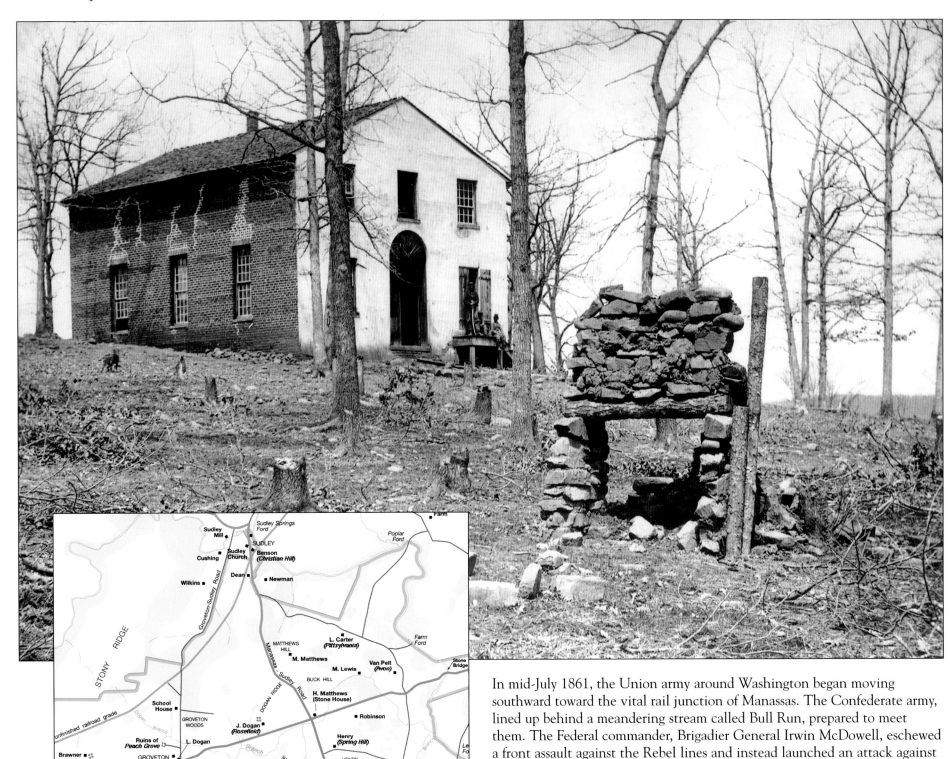

In mid-July 1861, the Union army around Washington began moving southward toward the vital rail junction of Manassas. The Confederate army, lined up behind a meandering stream called Bull Run, prepared to meet them. The Federal commander, Brigadier General Irwin McDowell, eschewed a front assault against the Rebel lines and instead launched an attack against his opponent's left flank. The bluecoats crossed Bull Run near a country chapel known as Sudley Church.

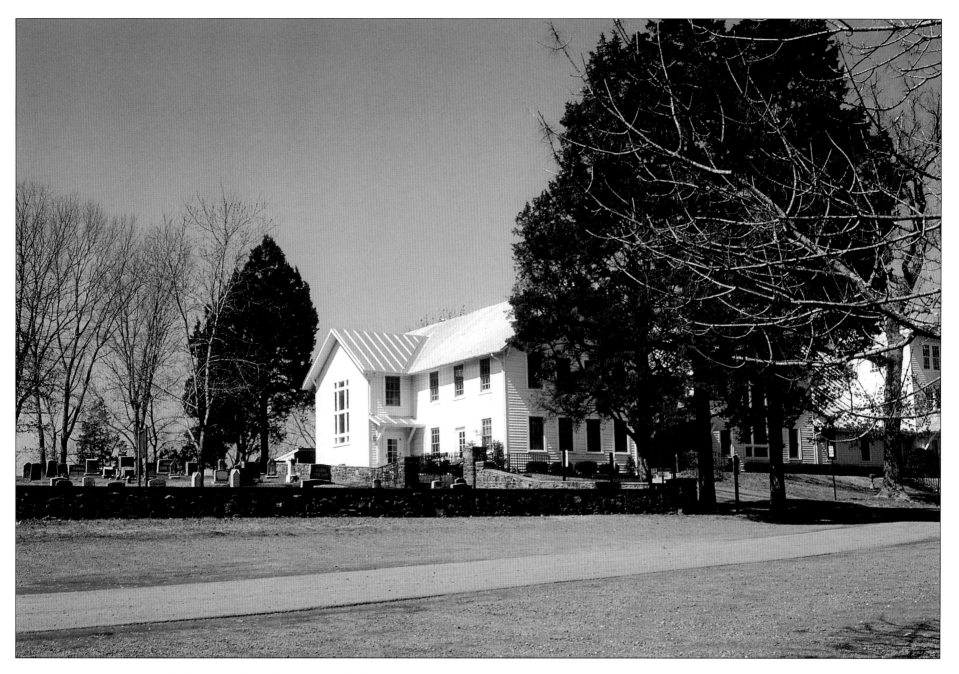

As the Union troops marched past Sudley Church toward the sounds of
battle, the small church became a hospital. Soon the numbers became
overwhelming, and many of the wounded were laid out in the yard. More
than 300 wounded Union soldiers were captured in and around the church at
the end of the battle. The church was so badly damaged during the war that
it was razed to the ground. The current church was built in 1922.

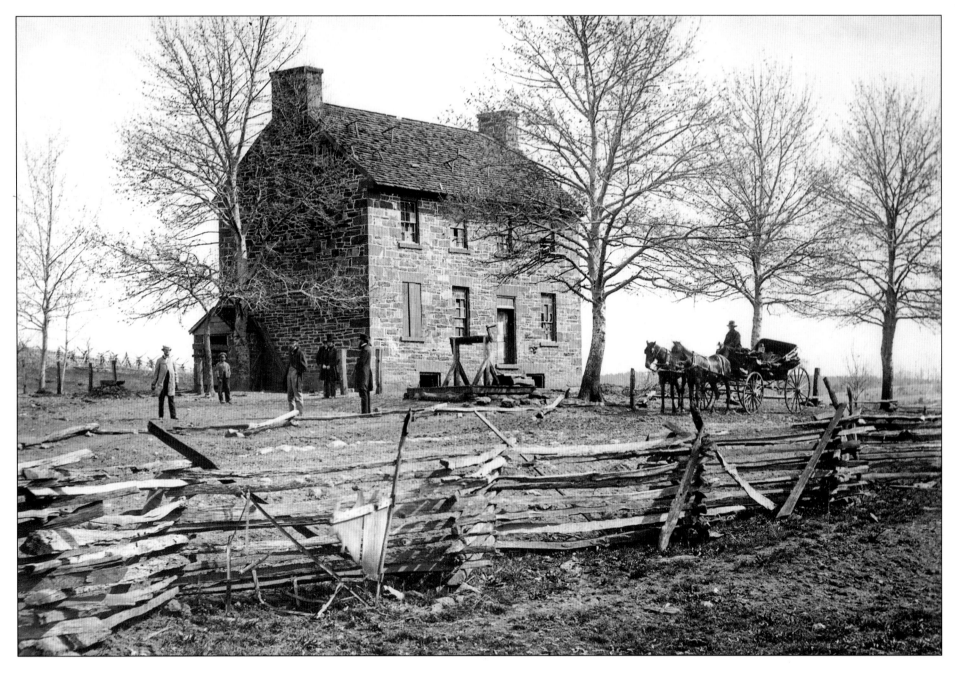

One of the most prominent landmarks on the Manassas battlefield is the Stone House, a country tavern located on the Warrenton Turnpike near its junction with Sudley Road. The seemingly victorious Union army surged past the house on July 21, 1861, as it attempted to finish off the remnants of the Confederate army on nearby Henry House Hill. As with most battlefield structures, the tavern was soon filled with the wounded.

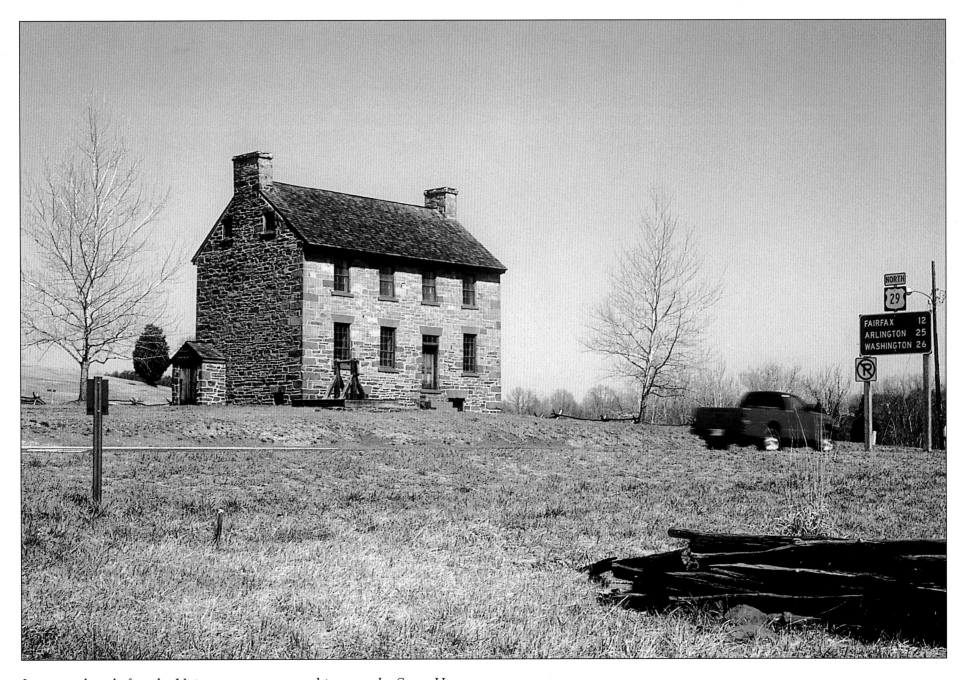

It was not long before the Union troops were marching past the Stone House again, this time in defeat. The house was soon captured by Virginian troops with fixed bayonets. One year later, the house would witness another battle and another Northern defeat. Following the Second Battle of Manassas, the tavern was used by Confederates to parole Federal prisoners. The house, still bearing the scars of the two battles, is today maintained by the National Park Service.

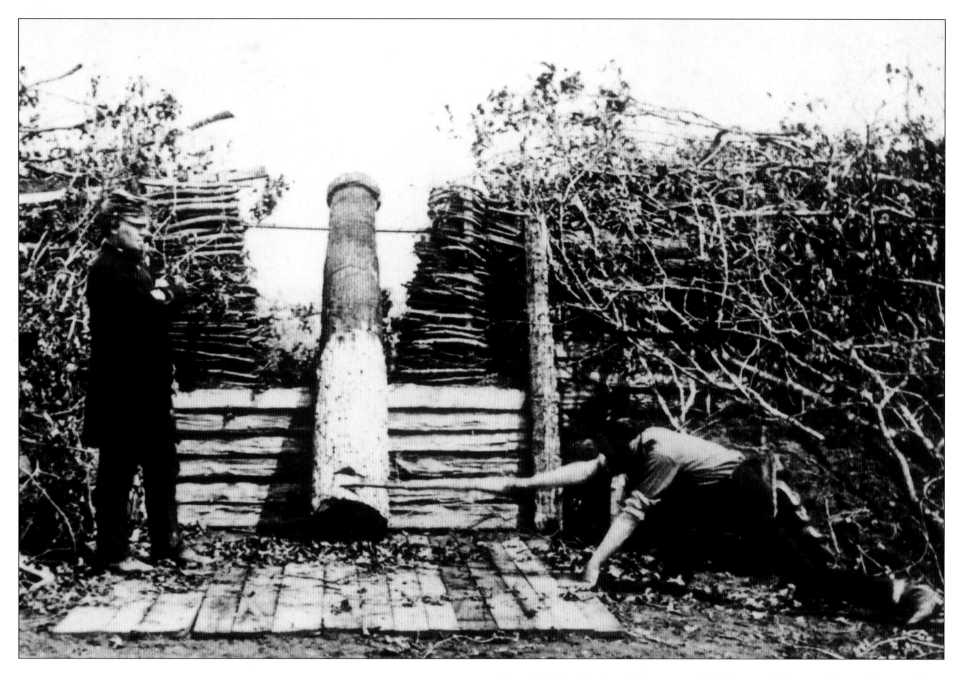

After the First Battle of Manassas, a lull descended upon the combatants in the east. The Union army returned to Washington to lick its wounds and build a more formidable force, soon designated the Army of the Potomac. Meanwhile, the victorious Confederate legions settled into camps around Centerville, where they would remain until March 1862. The Southerners also commenced building an extensive network of entrenchments to protect Manassas Junction.

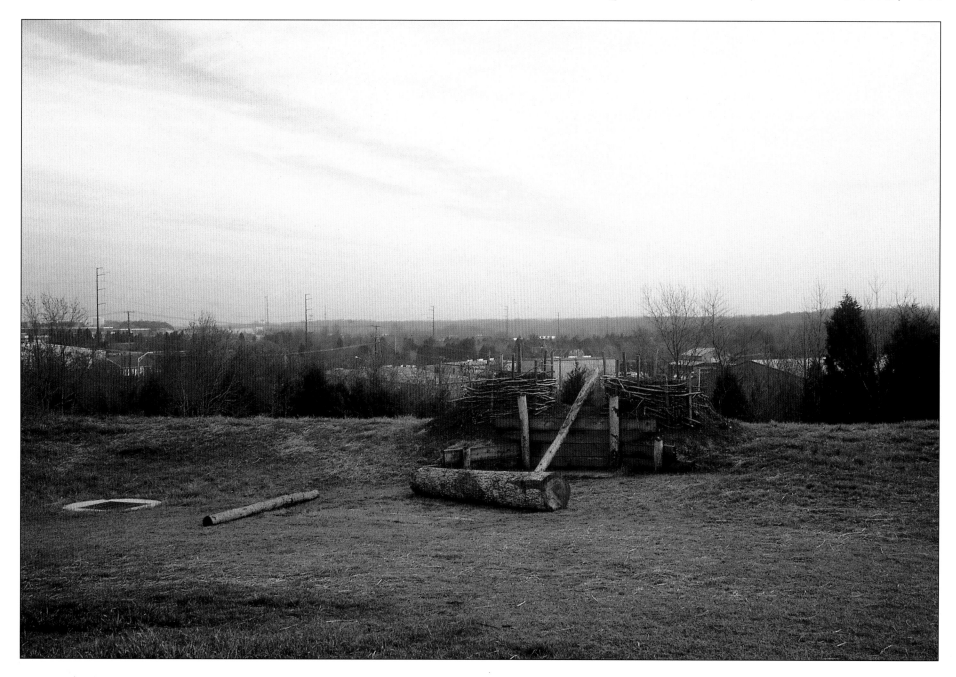

Despite the fearsome appearance of the earthworks, the Confederates simply did not have the heavy ordnance necessary to make the works impregnable. To compensate for their lack of real weapons, the inventive Rebels painted logs to look like cannons. These faux cannons were dubbed "Quaker guns" by the chagrined Northern press. Today, the location of the Quaker gun in the wartime image has disappeared, but a similar cannon has been reproduced at nearby Mayfield Fort.

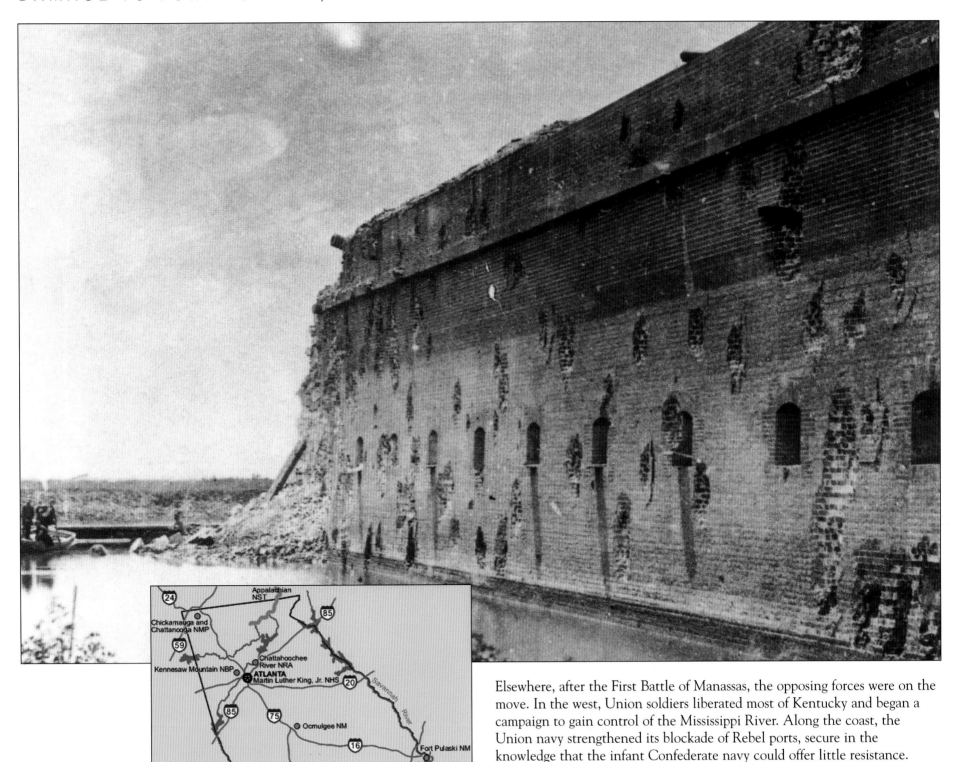

Elsewhere, after the First Battle of Manassas, the opposing forces were on the move. In the west, Union soldiers liberated most of Kentucky and began a campaign to gain control of the Mississippi River. Along the coast, the Union navy strengthened its blockade of Rebel ports, secure in the knowledge that the infant Confederate navy could offer little resistance. Combined with the army, the two services were able to restore Federal control over key coastal waterways.

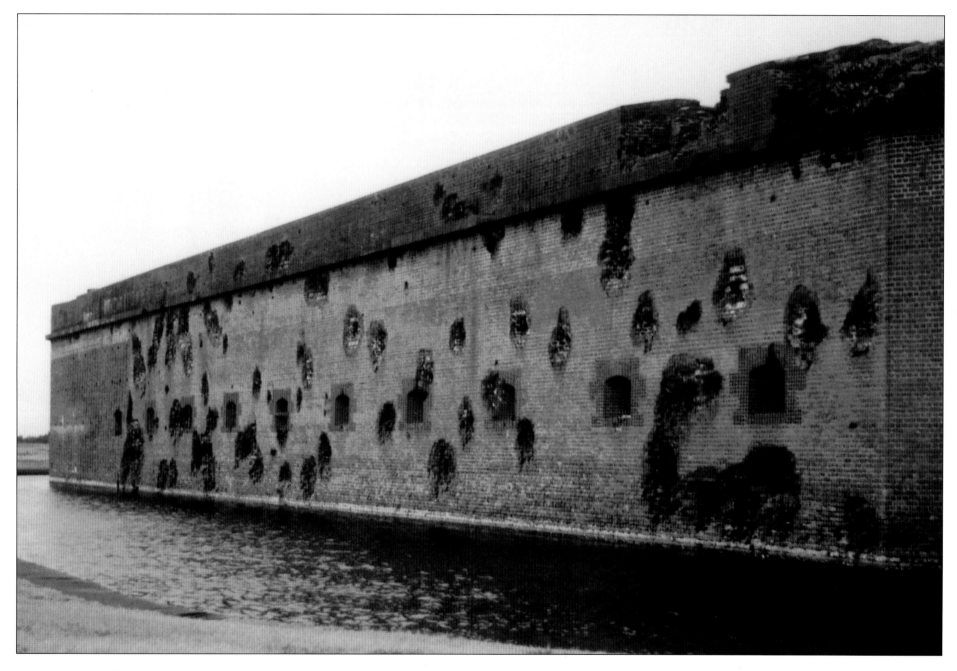

One of the first Union victories along the Atlantic coastline was at Fort Pulaski, a bastion guarding the Savannah River. The masonry fort, designed in part by then-Lieutenant Robert E. Lee, was considered nearly impregnable. However, in April 1862 a young Union engineer named Quincy Gilmore set out to prove rifled cannons had made masonry forts obsolete. The damage done to the fort by Gilmore's guns can still be seen today.

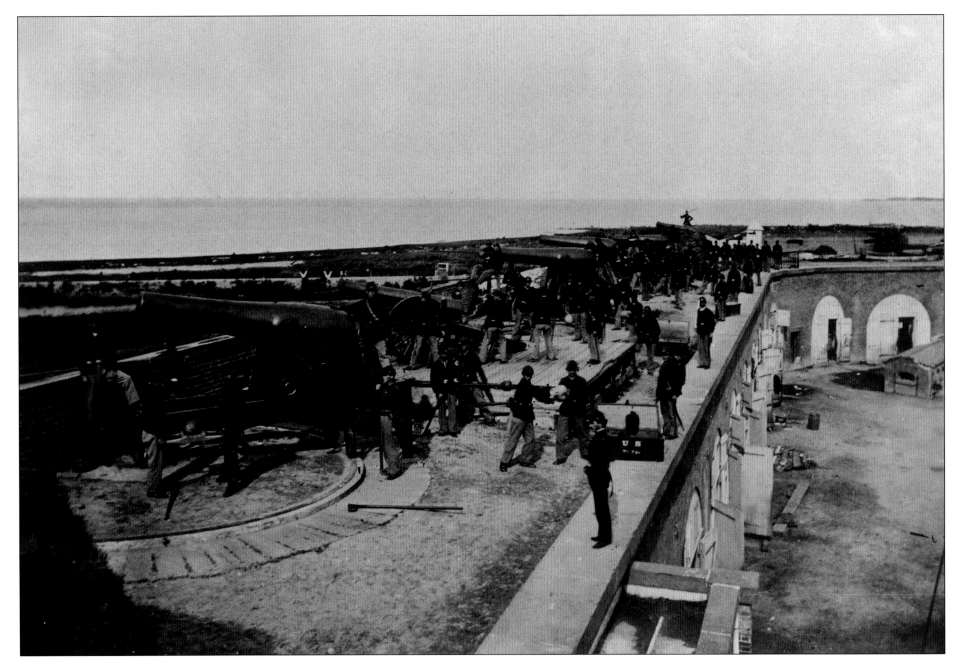

The once-mighty Fort Pulaski began to crumble under the unrelenting bombardment of 1862. In less than two days, several casemates were destroyed, and Pulaski's southeast wall was breached, making the fort vulnerable to attack by a Union assault party. Even worse, the breach meant that enemy gunners were able to fire directly upon the fort's powder magazine. Faced with the likely destruction of both the fort and its defenders, Fort Pulaski's commander chose to surrender.

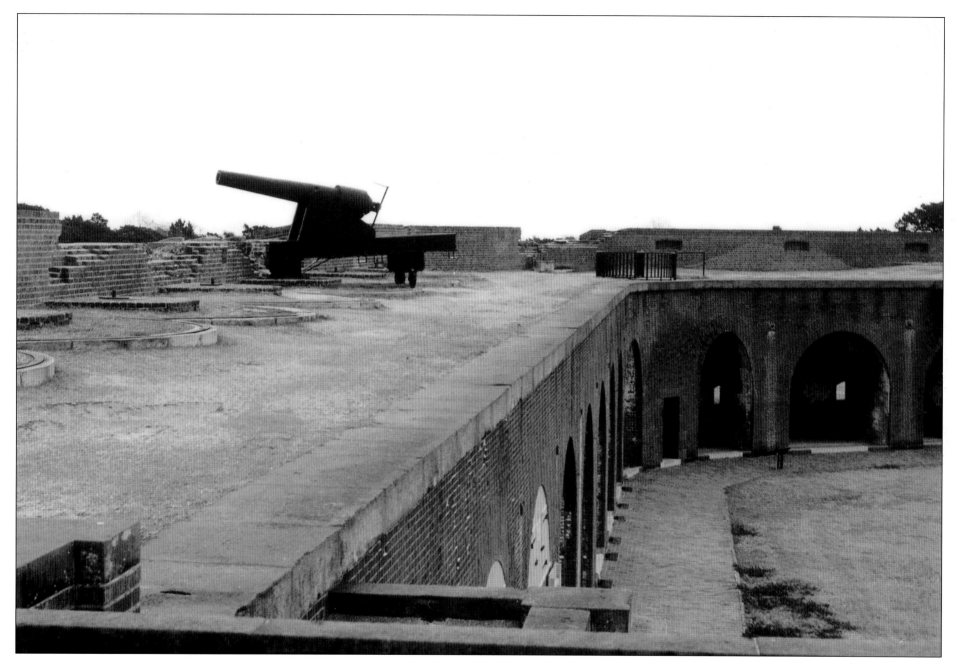

The fort's surrender was a major blow to Southern independence. Its capture allowed the Union navy to tighten its blockade and permitted the Union army to gradually gain control of key islands off the Georgia and South Carolina coast. For the remainder of the war, Fort Pulaski would be held by Union troops bored by the tedium of garrison duty. Today Fort Pulaski has been restored to its wartime appearance by the National Park Service.

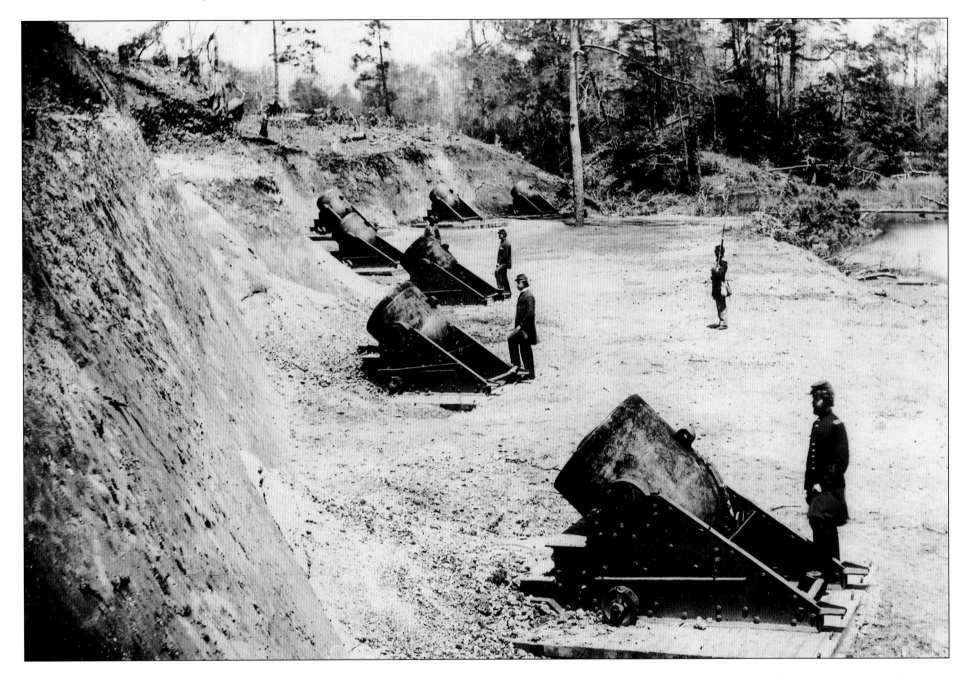

In April 1862, the Army of the Potomac began another campaign toward Richmond. Not overland, past the now-abandoned Confederate earthworks at Manassas, but by sea, toward the peninsula between the York and James Rivers. The Union army, numbering in excess of 100,000 men, began moving slowly up the peninsula toward the colonial port of Yorktown. As the Union host approached Yorktown, their advance was abruptly halted by a handful of Confederate gunners.

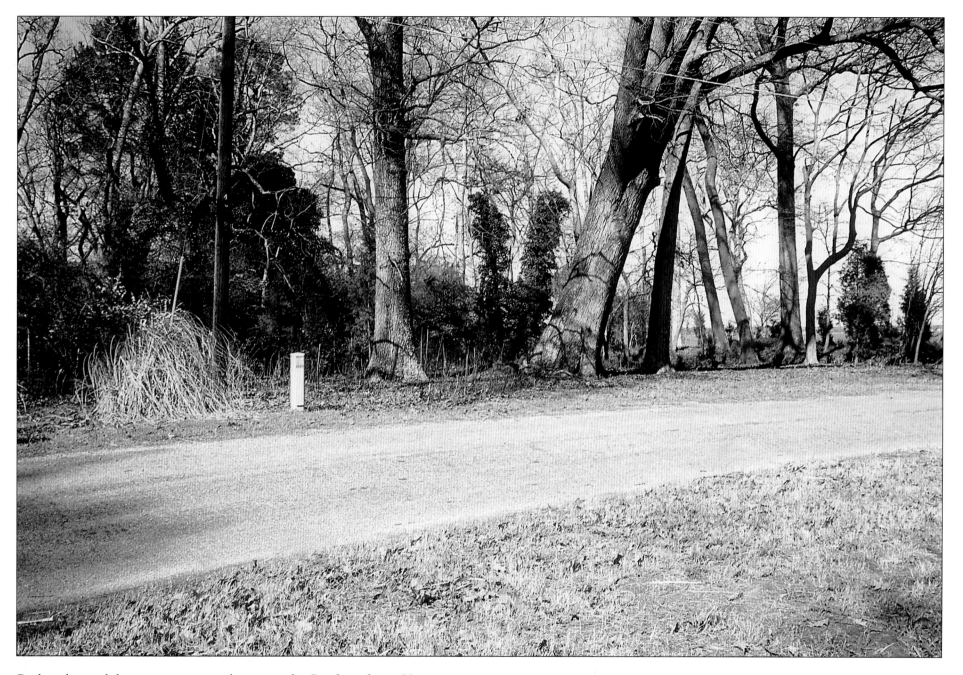

Rather than risk his men in an assault against the Southern lines, Union Major General George McClellan laid siege to Yorktown. He brought up heavy artillery, including the ten thirteen-inch mortars of Battery 4, manned by men of the 1st Connecticut Heavy Artillery. Today the location of Battery 4 is all but forgotten, obscured not just by brush but also by Yorktown's emphasis on its Revolutionary War history.

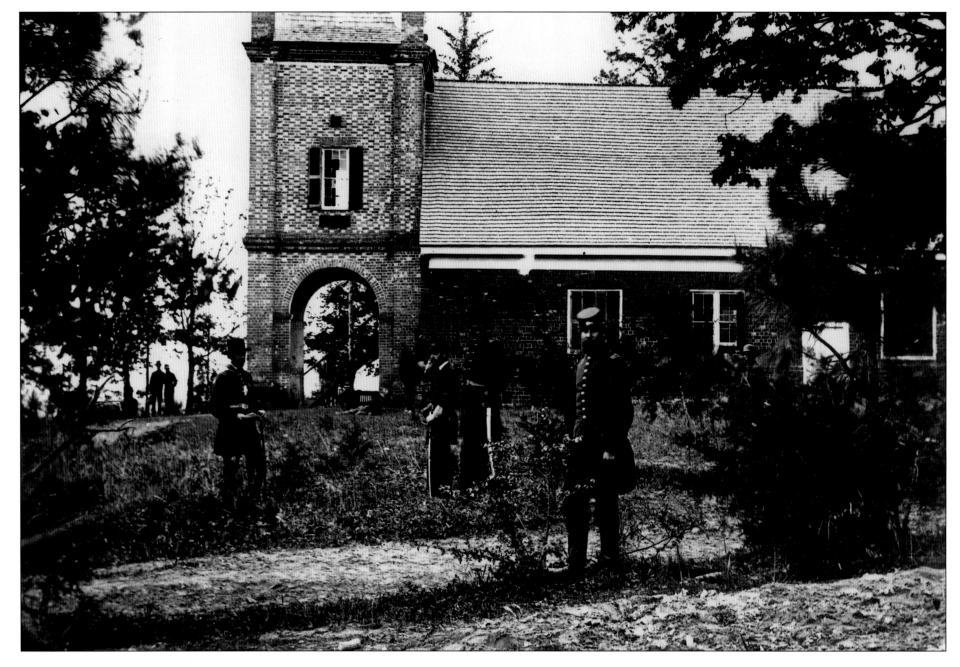

In May 1862, the Confederate commander, General Joseph Johnston, abandoned Yorktown and began retreating closer to Richmond. McClellan's army followed, eventually catching up with its adversary at Williamsburg on May 5. After a sharp rearguard action, the pursuit continued, with the Southern forces finally halting within sight of the spires of Richmond. The Union army began settling in for a siege, taking over several local buildings in the process.

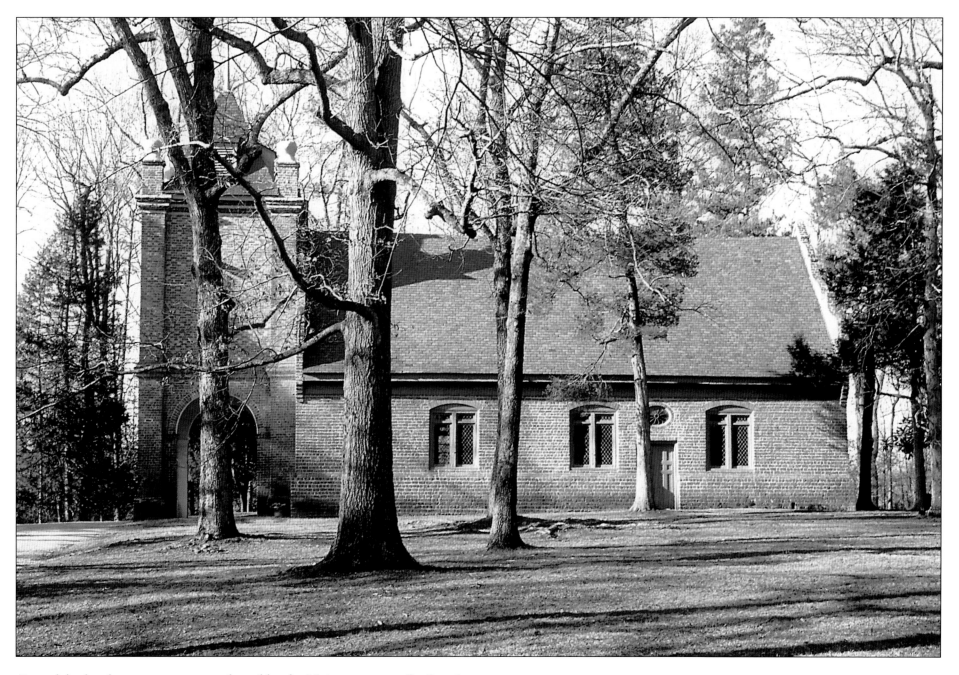

One of the local structures commandeered by the Union army was St. Peter's Church, the site of George and Martha Washington's wedding in 1759. During the Peninsula Campaign, the church was strategically located between the Chickahominy River and the Federal base at White House. The church grounds served as a bivouac for the Union Second Corps commander. Two years later, in June 1864, cavalry fights would break out nearby. Although damaged, the church survived the war.

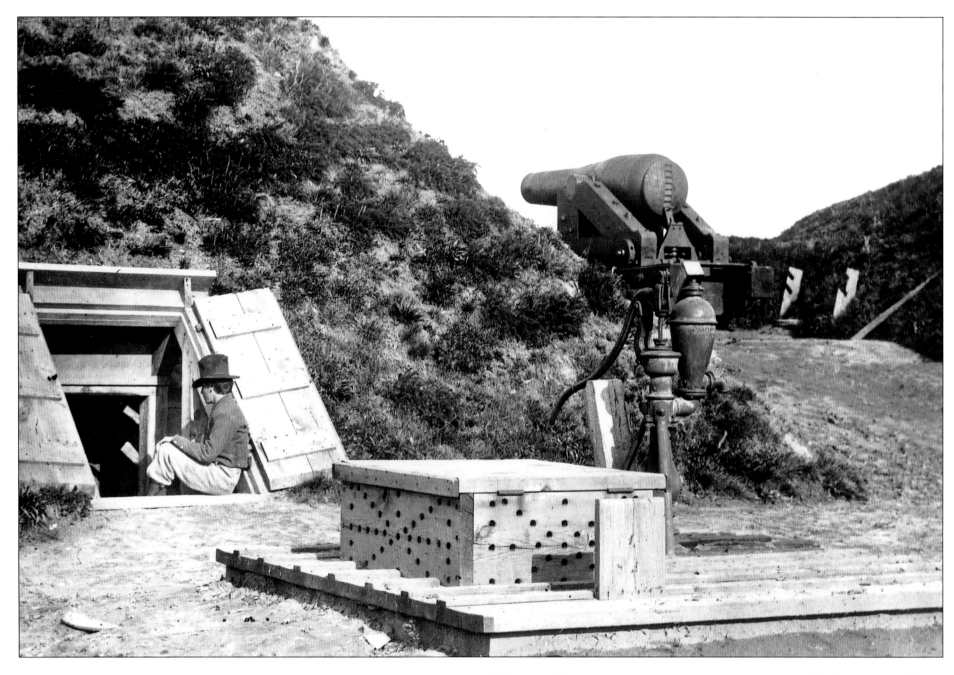

While the Union army moved up the peninsula toward Richmond in 1862, "Uncle Sam's webbed feet" were also busy trying to open the waterborne route to Richmond. Five Federal gunboats, including the famous ironclad U.S.S. *Monitor*, began steaming up the James River toward the Confederate capital. The *Monitor's* counterpart, the C.S.S. *Virginia* (formerly the *Merrimack*) had recently been scuttled, and little stood in the way of the Union task force and Richmond.

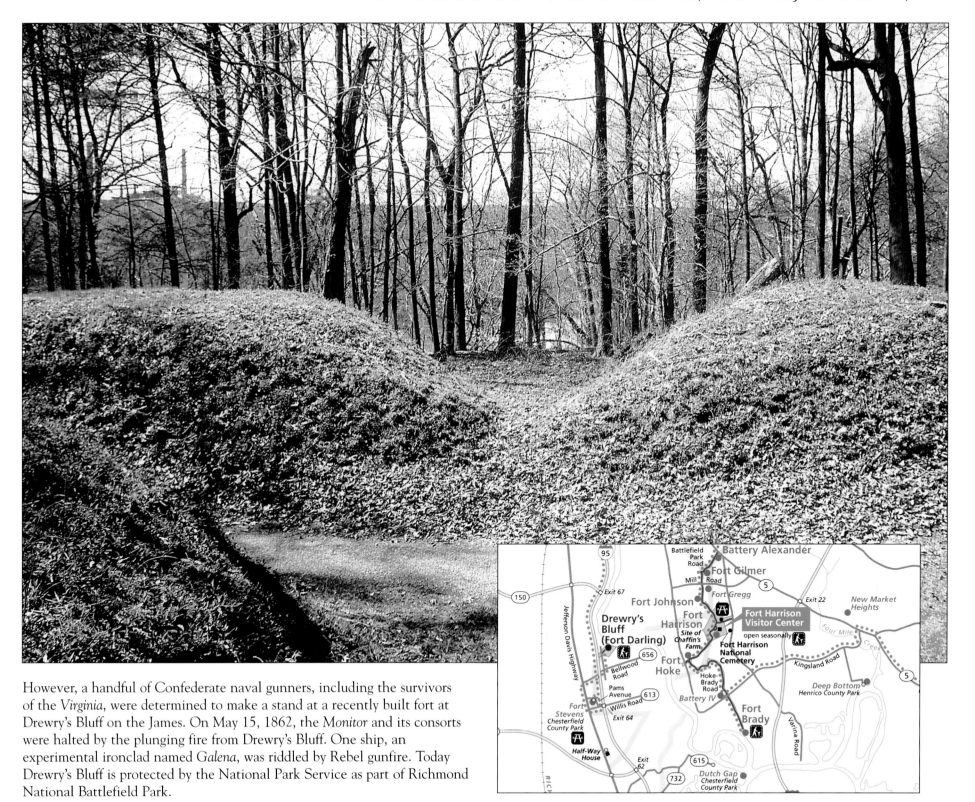

However, a handful of Confederate naval gunners, including the survivors of the *Virginia*, were determined to make a stand at a recently built fort at Drewry's Bluff on the James. On May 15, 1862, the *Monitor* and its consorts were halted by the plunging fire from Drewry's Bluff. One ship, an experimental ironclad named *Galena*, was riddled by Rebel gunfire. Today Drewry's Bluff is protected by the National Park Service as part of Richmond National Battlefield Park.

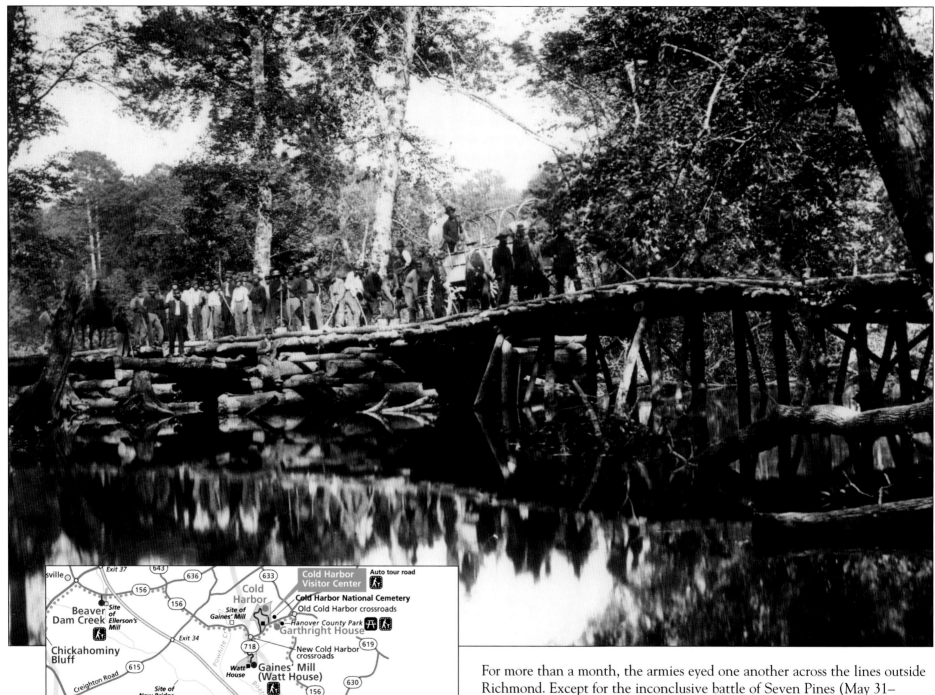

For more than a month, the armies eyed one another across the lines outside Richmond. Except for the inconclusive battle of Seven Pines (May 31–June 1, 1862) the opposing forces spent most of their time bridging rivers, bringing up reinforcements, and preparing for battle. Behind the gray lines, the new Confederate commander, General Robert E. Lee, was making plans to lift the siege. His strategy would make use of the Chickahominy River, which split the Federal army in two.

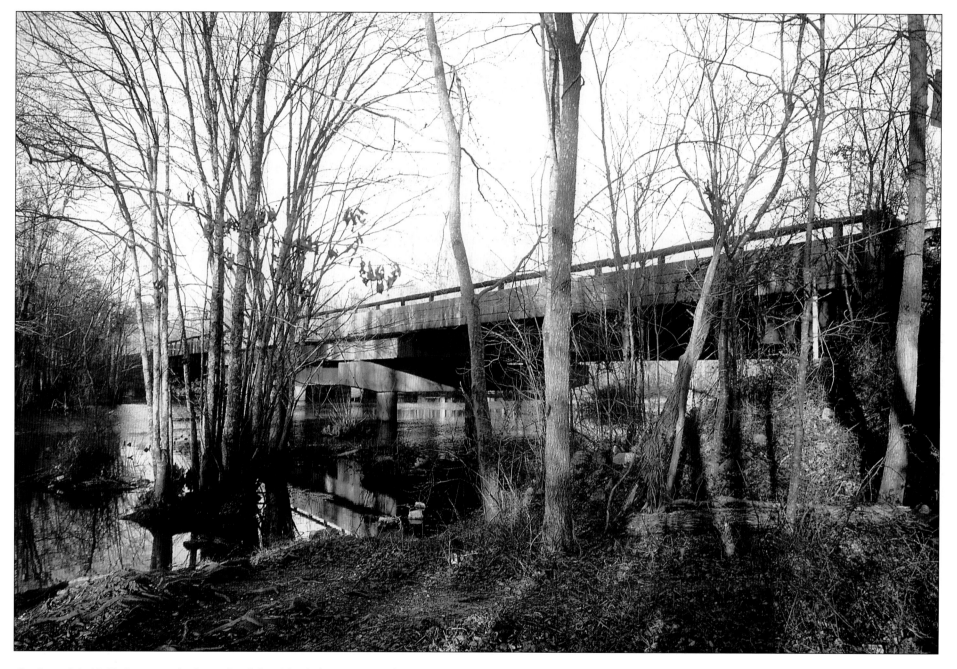

On June 26, 1862, Lee attacked north of the Chickahominy, catching McClellan's army off guard and forcing it to retreat. McClellan was compelled to evacuate his positions north of the river, destroying the bridges his engineers had constructed during the past four weeks. The damage to Grapevine Bridge would delay Confederate Major General Thomas "Stonewall" Jackson's pursuit long enough to enable the Union army to flee intact. Grapevine Bridge has since been replaced by a modern structure.

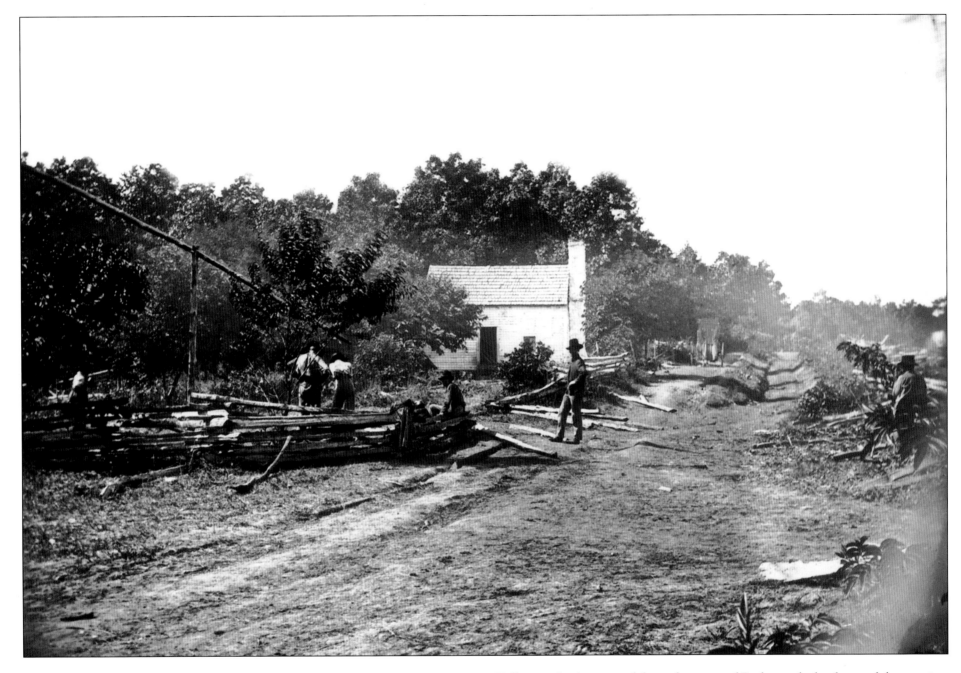

Following Lee's success lifting the siege of Richmond, the focus of the war in Virginia moved to Culpeper County. A new Union army, designated the Army of Virginia and commanded by General John Pope, began moving southward along the Orange and Alexandria Railroad. By August 1862, the Federals had occupied Culpeper and were threatening Richmond from the north. To counter this threat, Lee sent Stonewall Jackson to the scene to suppress Pope's forces.

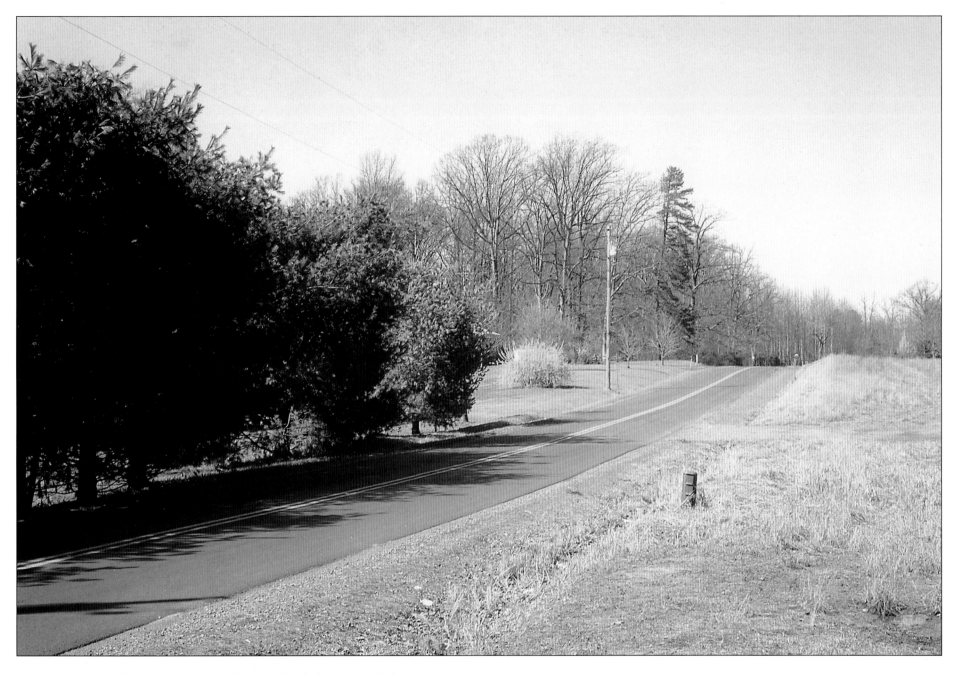

On August 9, 1862, Jackson attacked Pope's divided army at Cedar Mountain. Despite outnumbering his adversary two to one, Jackson's men were nearly driven from the field. At one point, the fighting became so desperate that Jackson was forced to draw his sword in order to rally his men—the only time during the war he would do so. Today, 152 acres of historic Cedar Mountain are protected by the Civil War Preservation Trust.

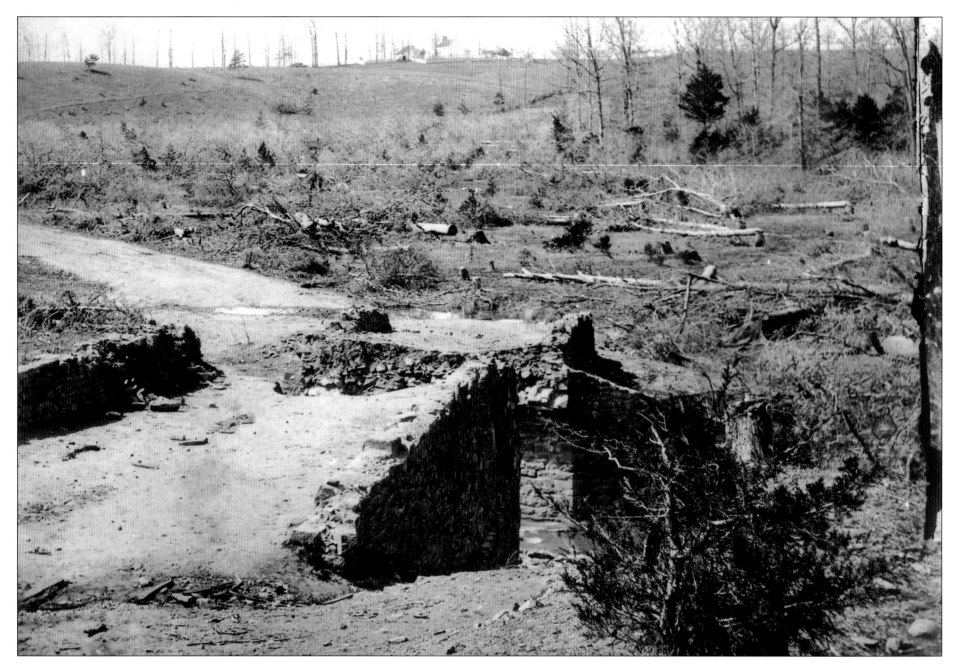

In the wake of Cedar Mountain, the armies again returned to Manassas, although it little resembled its bucolic appearance during the first battle in July 1861. Months of Confederate encampment, followed by Union occupation, had wreaked havoc on the battlefield. Few trees or fences remained, having been consumed for campfires or used as building materials, and many of the bridge crossings had been destroyed by retreating Southerners, only to be repaired by their counterparts in blue.

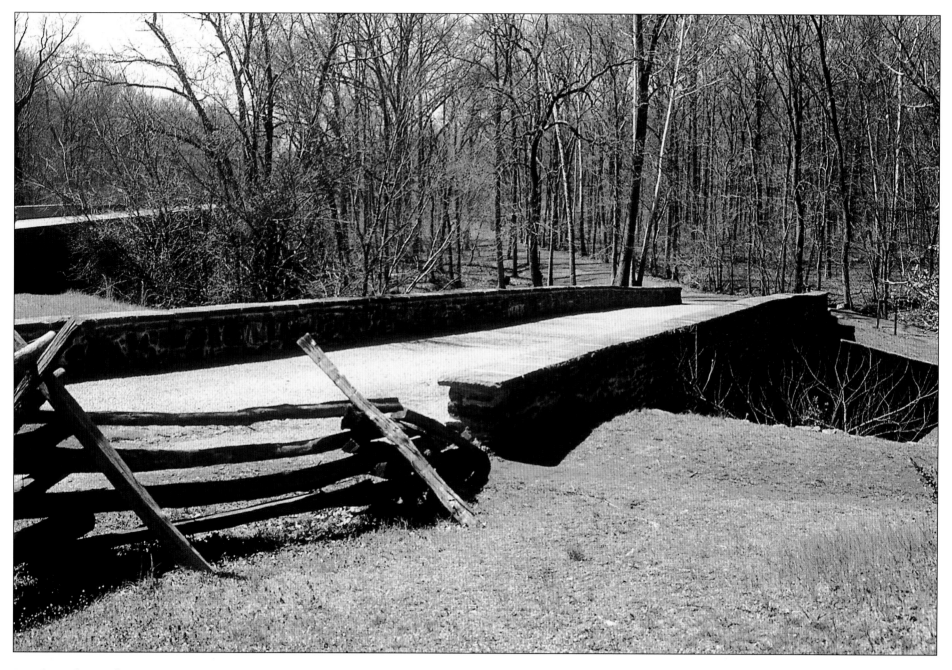

For three days in late August 1862, fighting would rage just west of Stone Bridge. General Pope, convinced he had Stonewall Jackson trapped, threw his army piecemeal against Jackson's line along an old abandoned railroad cut. In reality, it was Pope who had unwittingly stepped into a trap—a trap sprung when Confederate General James Longstreet's troops smashed into Pope's left flank, resulting in a defeat nearly as humiliating as at First Manassas.

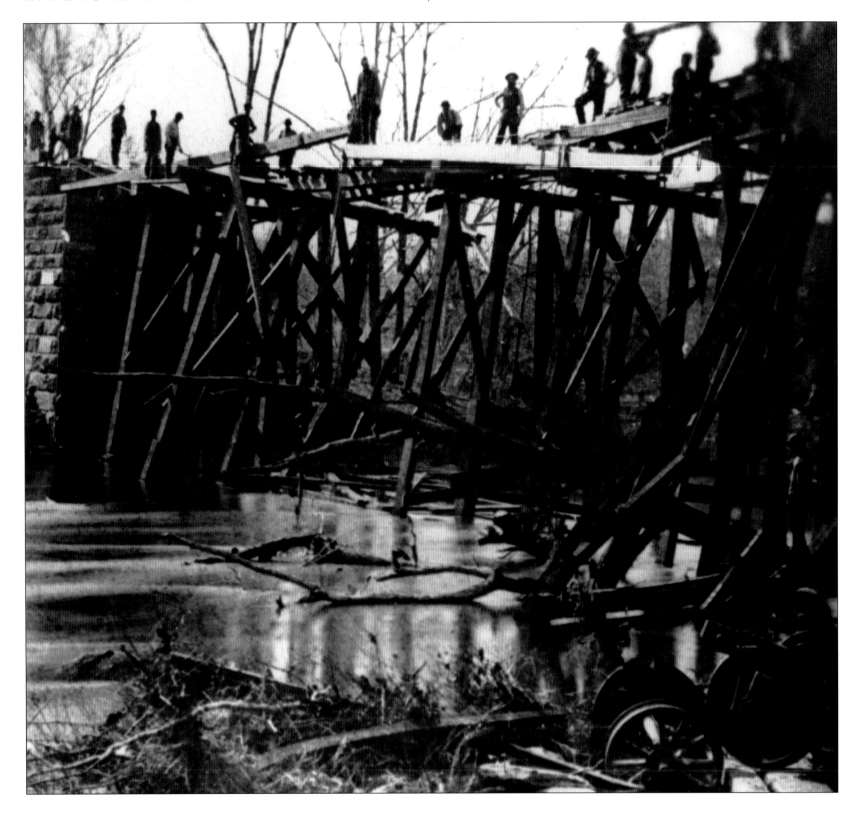

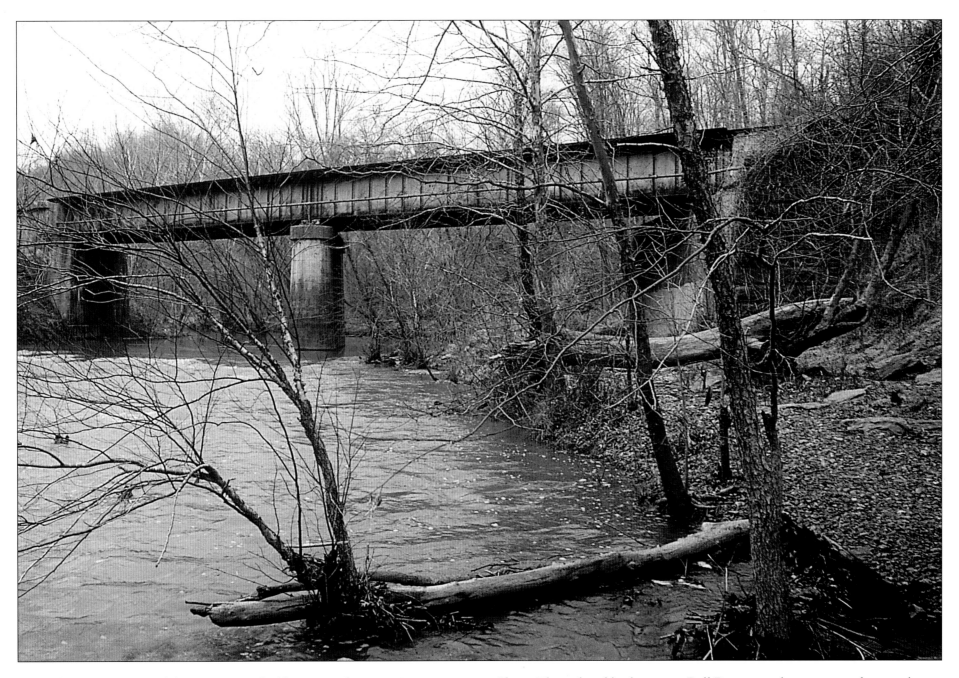

Left: The maneuvering of the armies wreaked havoc on the transportation network in Virginia. The Orange and Alexandria Railroad was a particular favorite of Rebel cavalry raiders, who would disrupt Federal supplies by burning its numerous bridges. Later in the war, when the regular Confederate cavalry was no longer able to penetrate into northern Virginia, guerilla units such as Colonel John Mosby's partisan rangers would continue to prey on the railroad.

Above: The railroad bridge across Bull Run seemed to get more than its share of attention. Despite numerous precautions, including the construction of a blockhouse, the bridge at Union Mills was destroyed and rebuilt seven times during the war. Only the efficiency of Union Colonel Herman Haupt's repair crews enabled the trains to keep supplying the Yankee army. Today a modern railroad bridge spans Bull Run at Union Mills, although the wartime stone abutments remain.

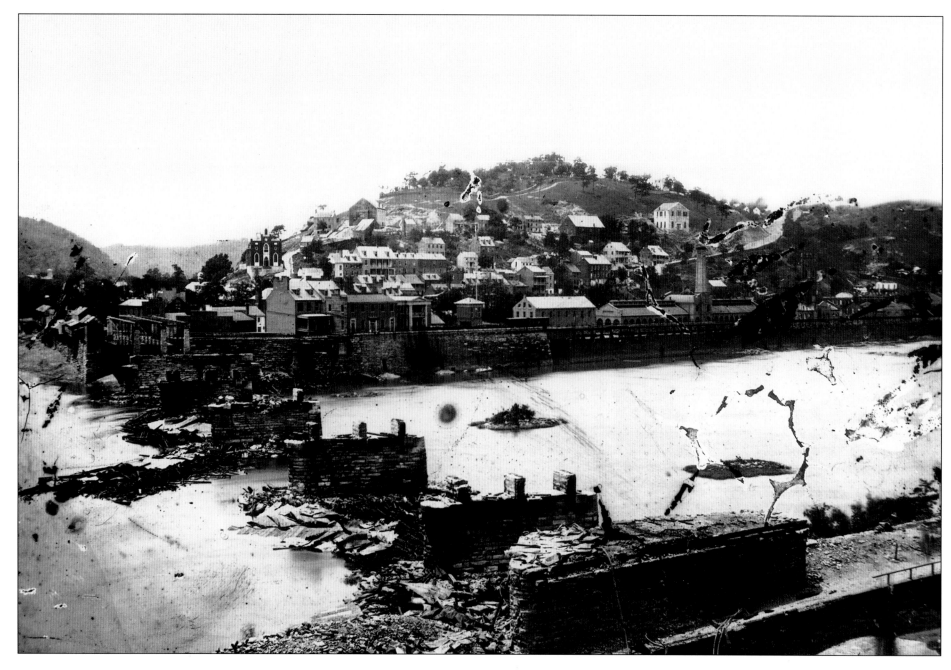

Scenic Harpers Ferry, situated at the confluence of the Potomac and Shenandoah Rivers, was once described by an admiring Thomas Jefferson as "worth a voyage across the Atlantic." Two years prior to the war, abolitionist John Brown attacked the U.S. Arsenal at Harpers Ferry, with the intent of arming Virginia's slaves. Although unsuccessful, Brown's attempt to foment a slave rebellion inflamed passions on both sides, making a compromise between the North and South impossible.

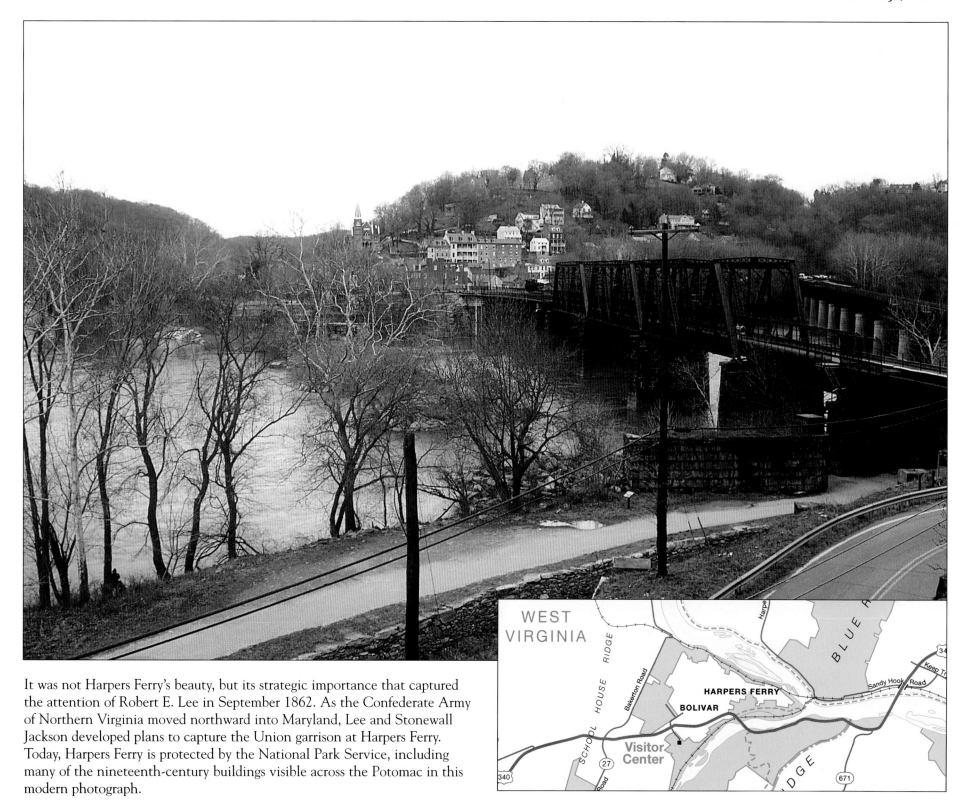

It was not Harpers Ferry's beauty, but its strategic importance that captured the attention of Robert E. Lee in September 1862. As the Confederate Army of Northern Virginia moved northward into Maryland, Lee and Stonewall Jackson developed plans to capture the Union garrison at Harpers Ferry. Today, Harpers Ferry is protected by the National Park Service, including many of the nineteenth-century buildings visible across the Potomac in this modern photograph.

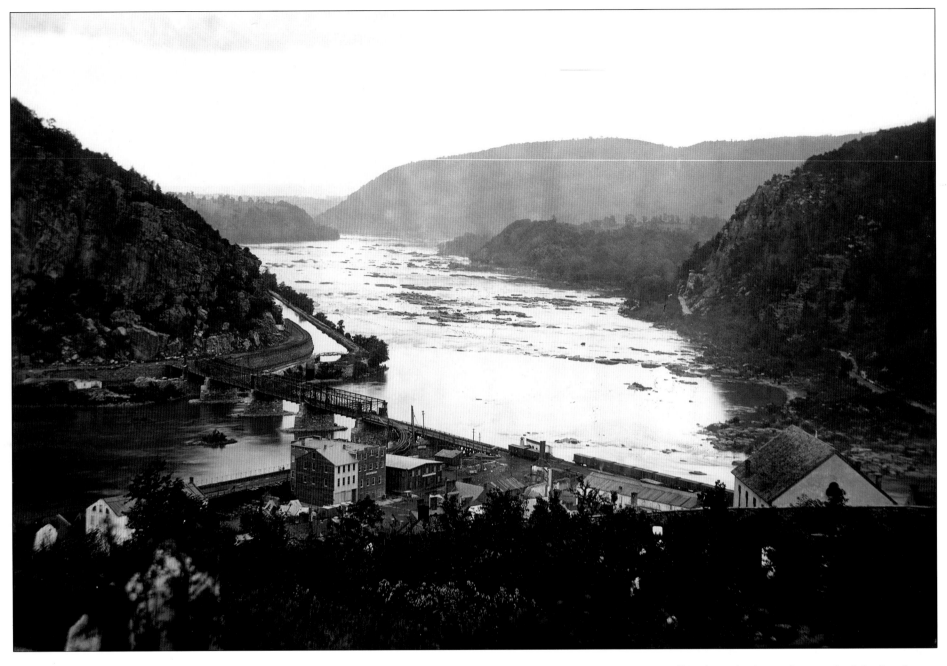

By September 13, 1862, Stonewall Jackson had seized control of the heights encircling Harpers Ferry. Jackson, employing the artillery tactics he once taught at the Virginia Military Institute, threw shell after shell into the beleaguered village. On September 15, the garrison commander, Colonel Nelson Miles, surrendered, only to be mortally wounded in the final salvo. More than 12,500 Union troops were forced to capitulate, the largest mass surrender in U.S. Army history until World War II.

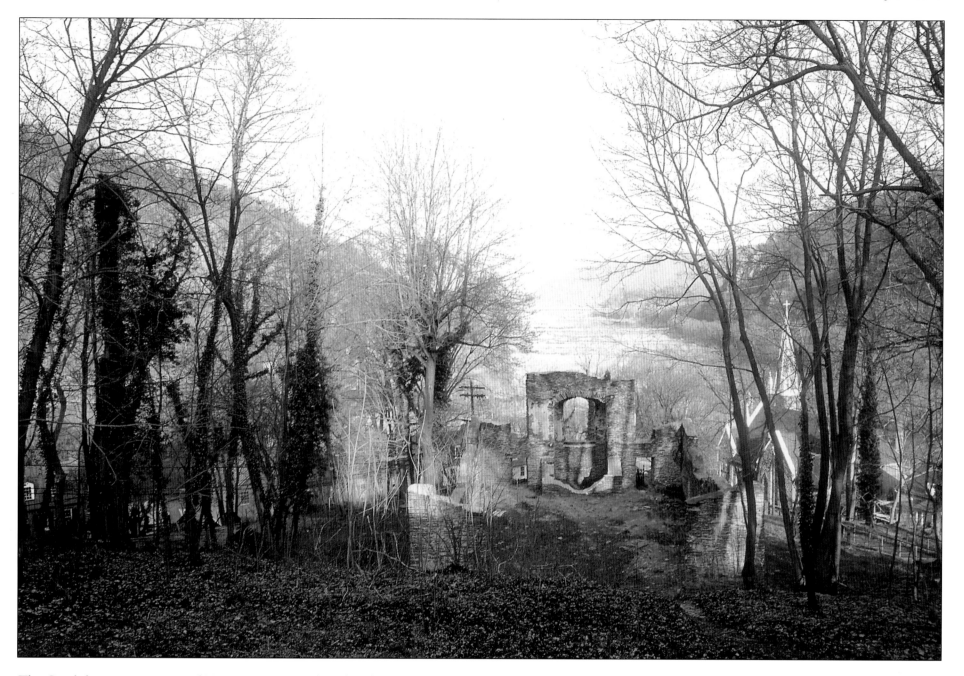

The Confederate occupation of Harpers Ferry was short lived. Less than a week after the surrender, the town and battlefield were reoccupied by Union troops who would remain for the rest of the war. Today Harpers Ferry National Historical Park includes key portions of the wartime battlefield, including Maryland and Loudoun Heights, seen looming in the distance. In the foreground are the ruins of St. Johns Episcopal Church.

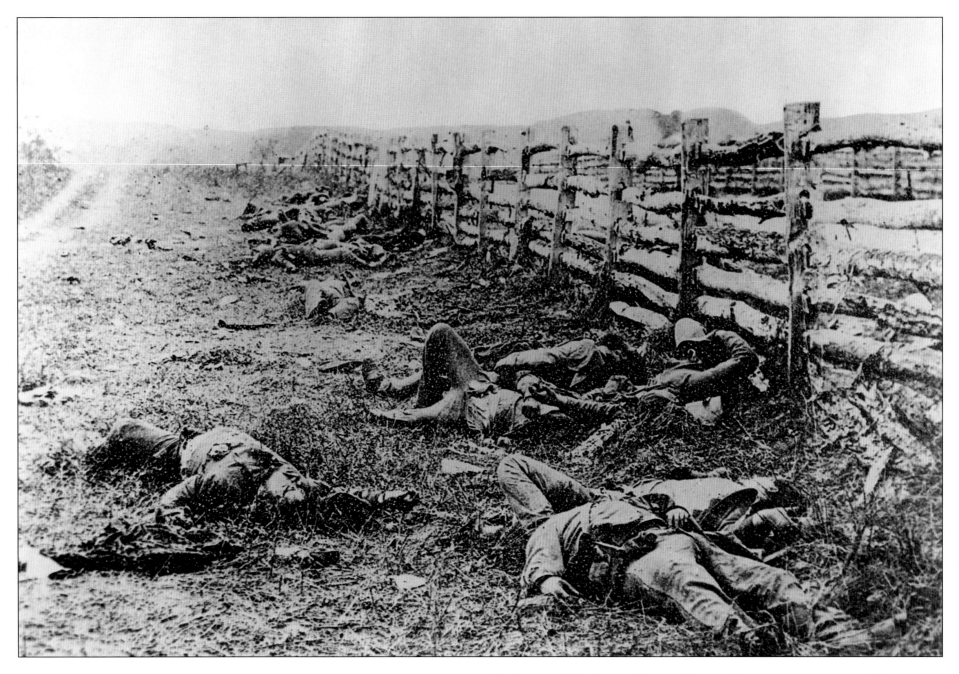

As the guns fell silent at Harpers Ferry, a far more sanguineous clash was brewing along Antietam Creek near Sharpsburg, Maryland. The Battle of Antietam, fought on September 17, 1862, would be the bloodiest day in American history. The two sides inflicted 22,000 casualties on each other during the course of the day, including between 3,600 and 4,700 dead and mortally wounded.

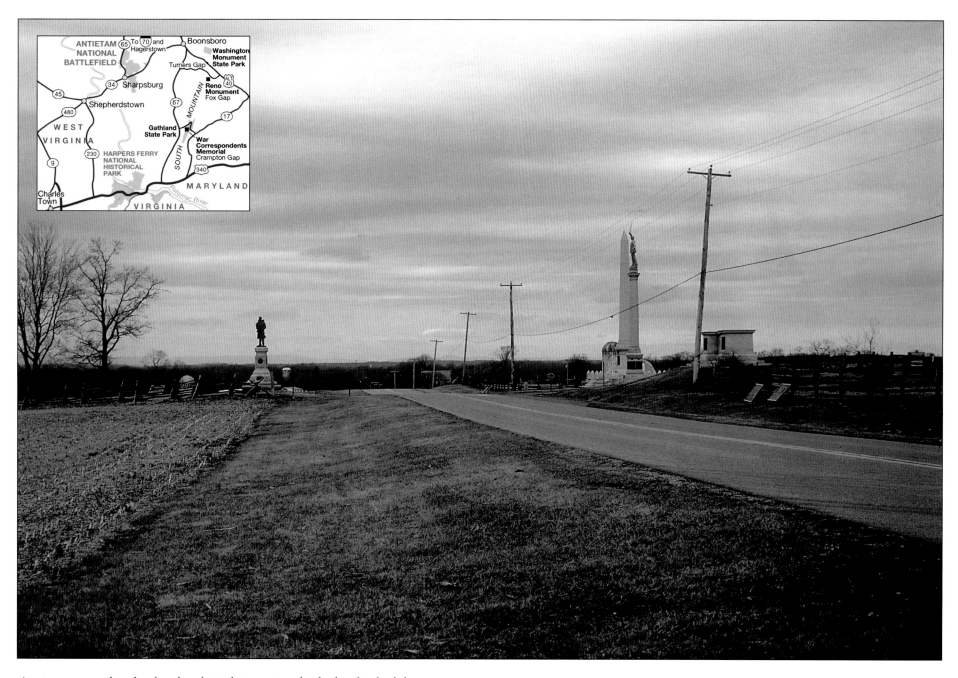

Antietam was also the first battle in history in which the dead of the battlefield were substantially photographed. Some of the first photographs were taken beside the old Hagerstown Pike, where fighting raged in the early morning hours of September 17, 1862. In this vicinity, Stonewall Jackson's command struggled against repeated attacks by three separate Union army corps. Today the site is protected as part of Antietam National Battlefield.

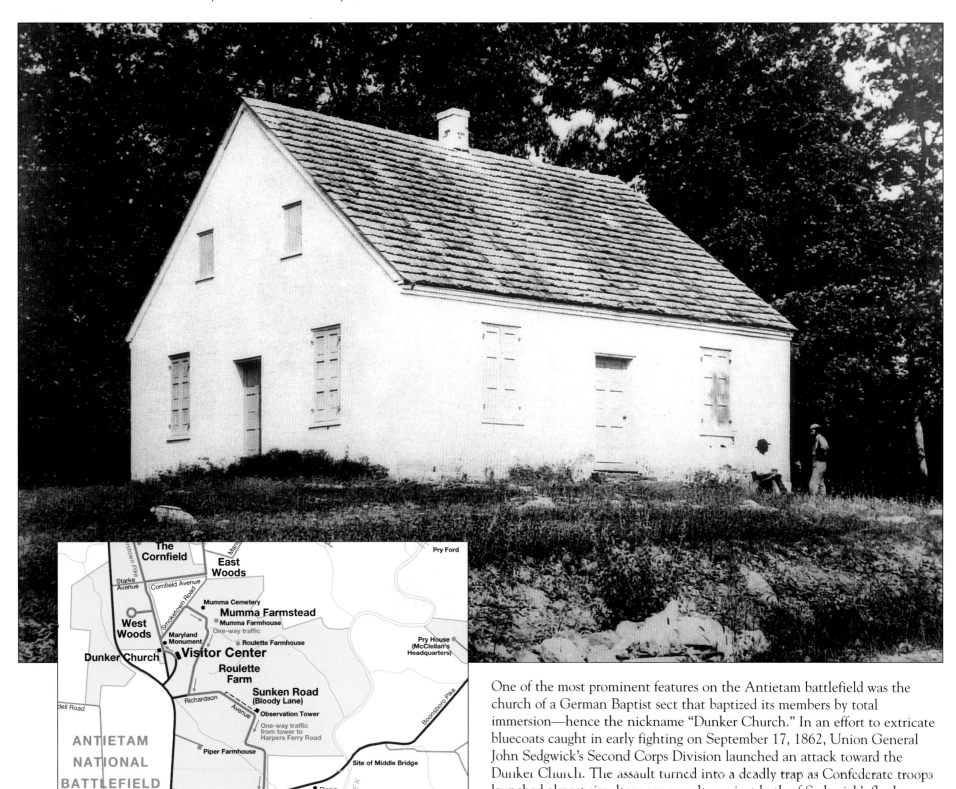

The map shows:
The Cornfield, East Woods, Pry Ford, Starke Avenue, Cornfield Avenue, Smoketown Road, Hagerstown Pike, Mumma Cemetery, Mumma Farmstead, Mumma Farmhouse, One-way traffic, Roulette Farmhouse, West Woods, Maryland Monument, Pry House (McClellan's Headquarters), Dunker Church, Visitor Center, Roulette Farm, Sunken Road (Bloody Lane), Observation Tower, Richardson Avenue, One-way traffic from tower to Harpers Ferry Road, Mandell Road, ANTIETAM NATIONAL BATTLEFIELD, Piper Farmhouse, Boonsboro Pike, Site of Middle Bridge, Picnic, Antietam Creek

One of the most prominent features on the Antietam battlefield was the church of a German Baptist sect that baptized its members by total immersion—hence the nickname "Dunker Church." In an effort to extricate bluecoats caught in early fighting on September 17, 1862, Union General John Sedgwick's Second Corps Division launched an attack toward the Dunker Church. The assault turned into a deadly trap as Confederate troops launched almost simultaneous assaults against both of Sedgwick's flanks.

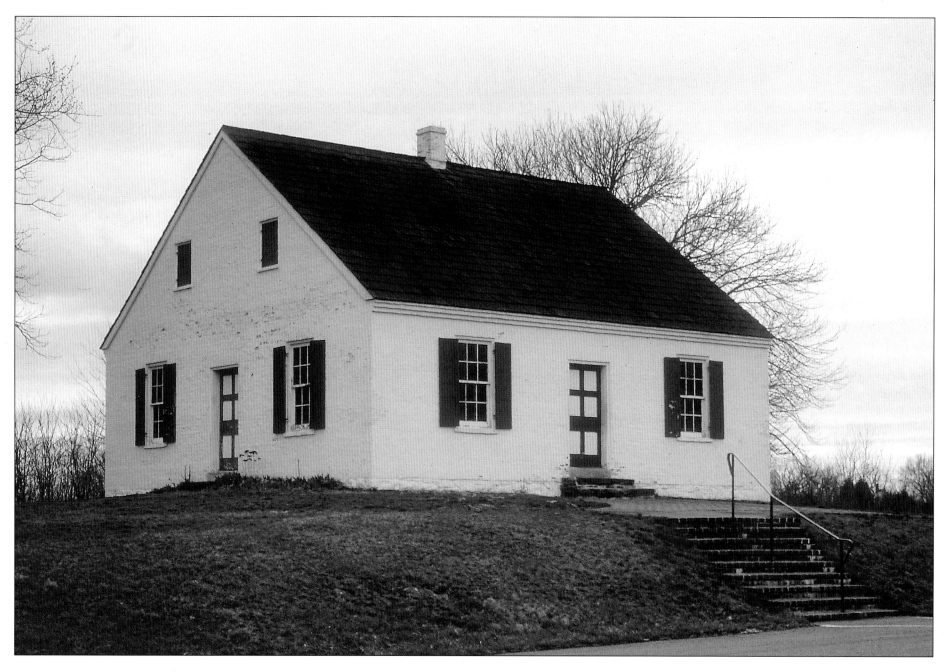

Despite the fierceness of the attacks against Sedgwick, the division retired in good order. The Second Corps historian would later note that "not a color is left to become a trophy of that bloody fight." The bullet-scarred Dunker Church would also survive the battle, only to fall prey to Mother Nature in 1921. However, the church's bricks were saved and became part of a new Dunker Church, rebuilt in time for the battle's centennial in 1962.

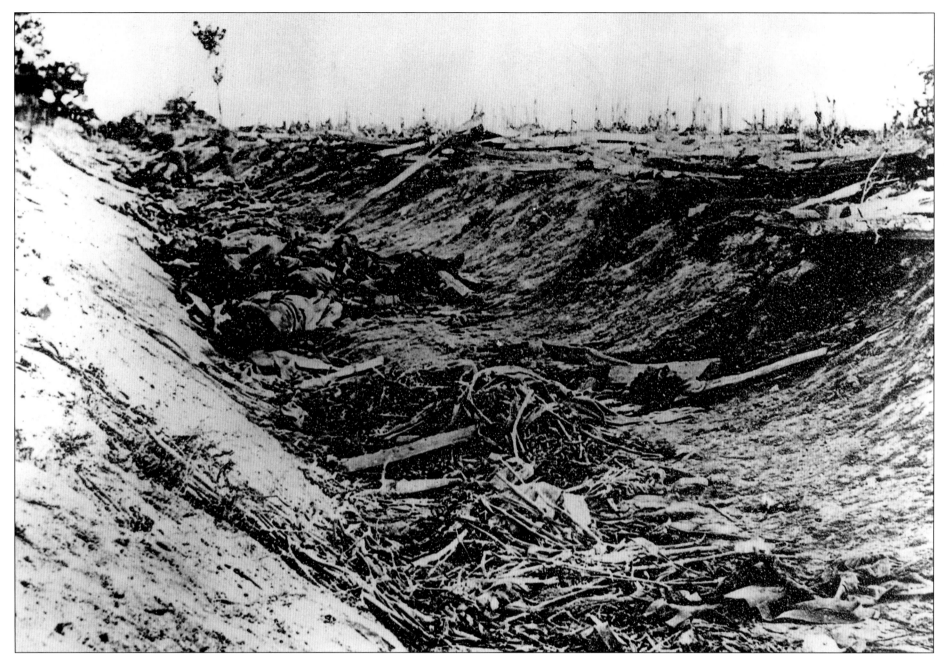

The Battle of Antietam was fought in phases that reflected the piecemeal attacks ordered by McClellan, the Union commander defeated by Lee a few months earlier on the Virginia Peninsula. The focus of the second phase of the battle, fought by elements of the Second Corps, was a sunken country road that Confederates under General Daniel Harvey Hill were using as a makeshift entrenchment. The repeated assaults against the road would forever earn it the moniker "Bloody Lane."

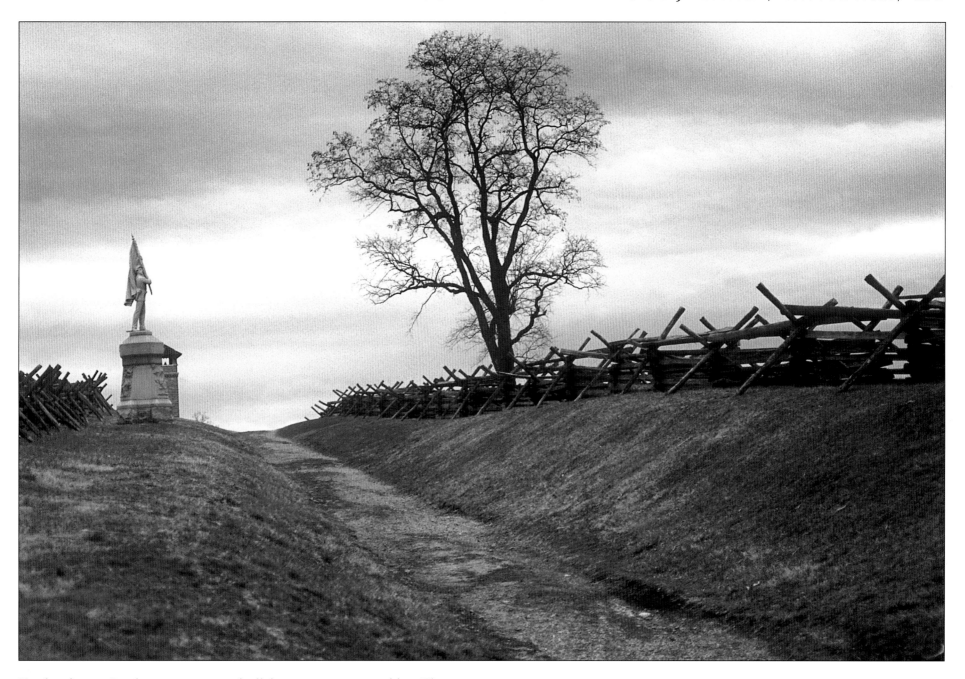

For four hours, Southern troops staved off their counterparts in blue. The repeated charges gradually thinned the Confederate ranks, and the sunken road became filled with the dead and wounded. Eventually, the weight of the Union assault broke the Rebel line, opening a path to Lee's rear. However, the exhausted Northerners failed to grasp the opportunity. Today the once blood-soaked lane is dotted with markers and monuments that tell the tale of the struggle waged there.

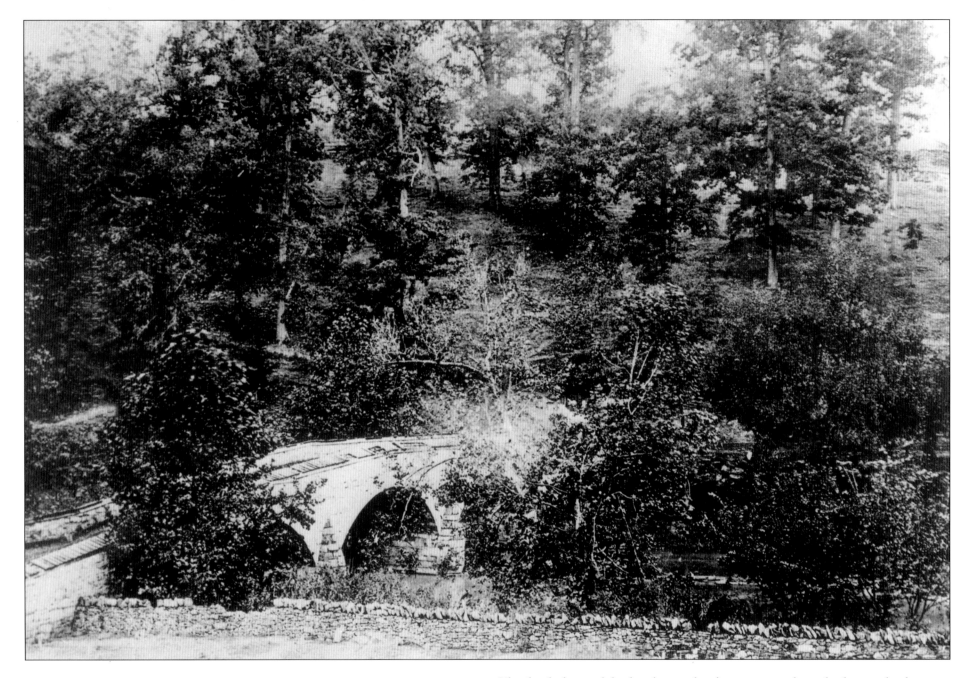

The final phase of the battle was fought over a triple-arched stone bridge across Antietam Creek. Here, Union General Ambrose Burnside's command was confronted by a handful of Georgian troops positioned on a bluff overlooking the bridge. Despite the enormous numerical superiority of the Federal forces, it would take Burnside nearly four hours to capture the bridge and the heights beyond. The bridge is today known as "Burnside Bridge."

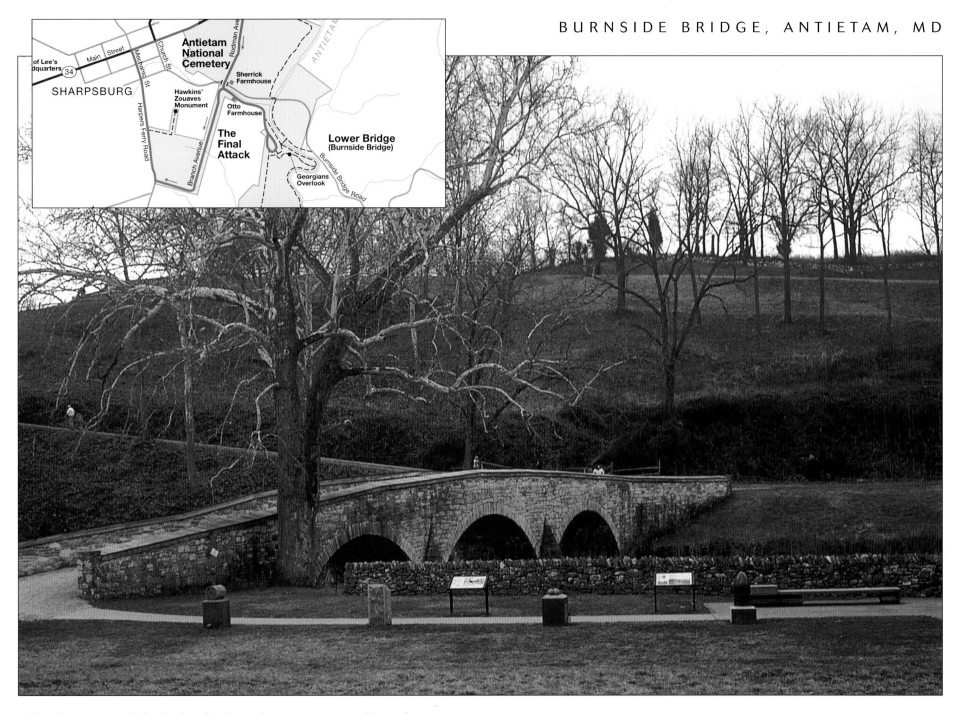

After the capture of the bridge that bears his name, victory lay within Burnside's grasp. However, rather than seize the opportunity, Burnside dawdled for two hours, giving Lee time to bring up badly needed reinforcements. The repulse of Burnside's belated attack brought the Battle of Antietam to an end. Two days later, Lee withdrew his battered but intact army across the Potomac, terminating his first invasion of the North.

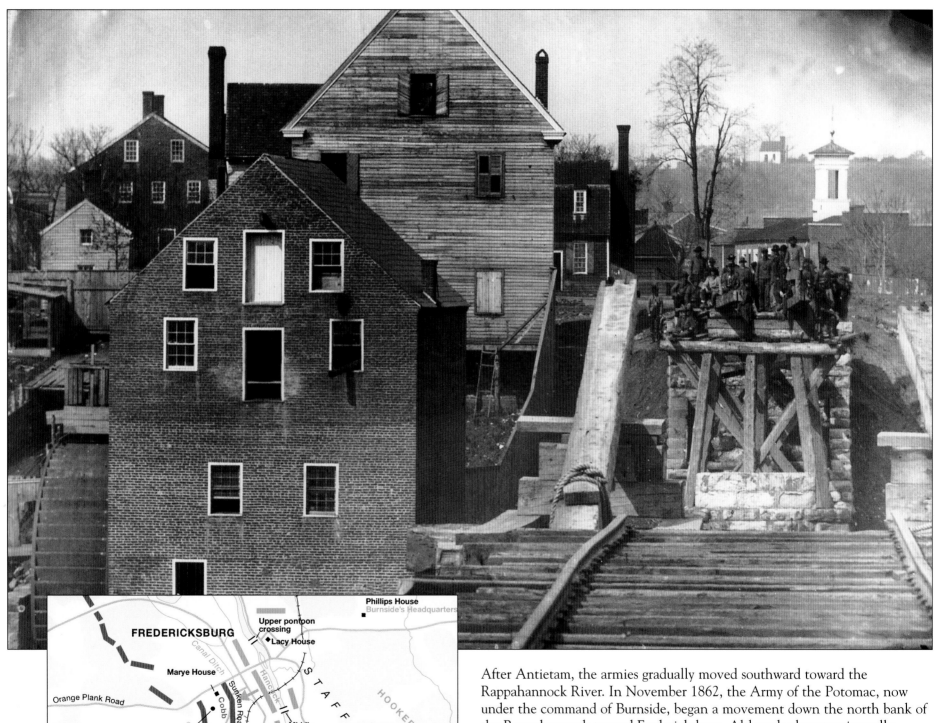

After Antietam, the armies gradually moved southward toward the Rappahannock River. In November 1862, the Army of the Potomac, now under the command of Burnside, began a movement down the north bank of the Rappahannock toward Fredericksburg. Although almost universally considered a mediocre general, both by historians and contemporaries, Burnside was actually able to steal a march on Lee, arriving at Fredericksburg well before any Southerners arrived to defend it.

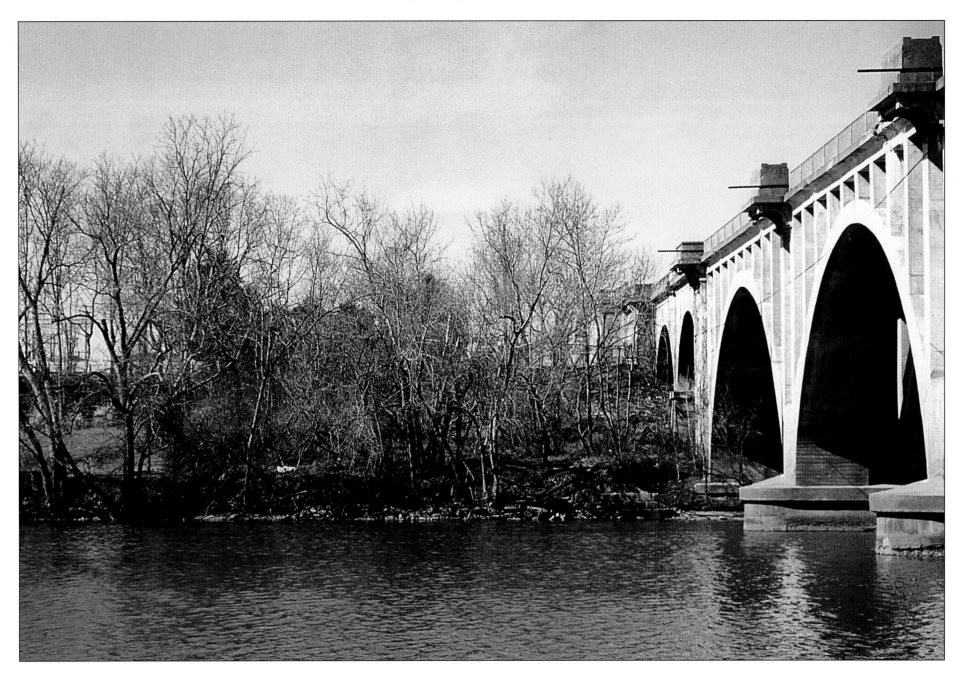

The bridges into Fredericksburg were destroyed, but the Rappahannock was fordable at several points. There was nothing stopping the Union host from taking the town—except the fears of the commander on the scene, who was worried that his troops would be trapped on the south side of the river in the event of a sudden storm. The result was that the Union troops simply sat on the north bank watching their gray-clad enemy march into Fredericksburg unopposed.

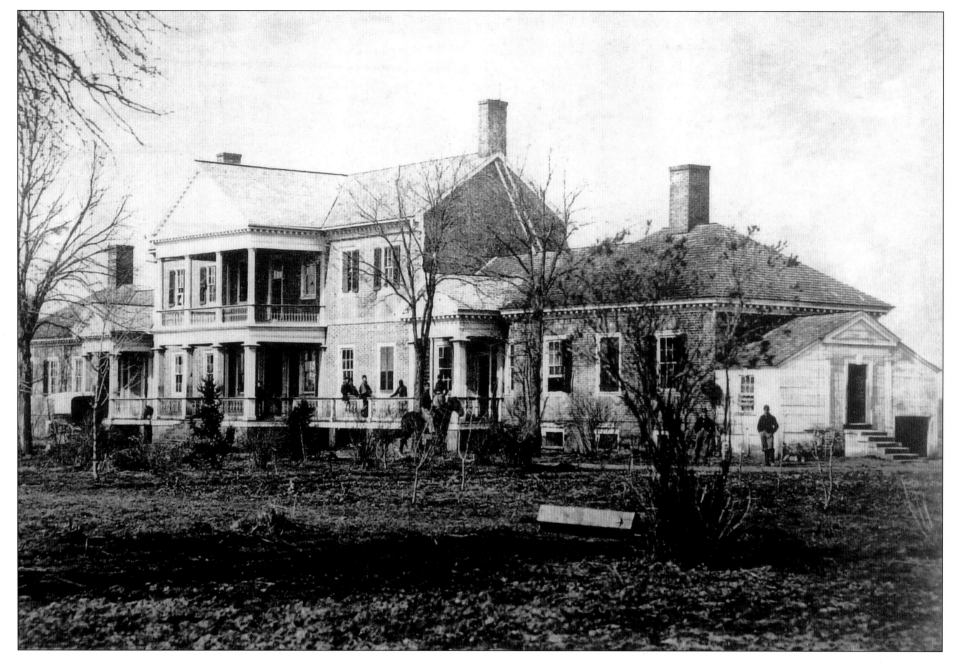

One of the finest views of Fredericksburg could be found at Chatham, the Georgian mansion owned by Confederate Major J. Horace Lacy. The house served as headquarters for a multitude of Union generals throughout the war. During the Battle of Fredericksburg, the house was headquarters for the Federal army's Right Grand Division. After the battle, the mansion became a hospital where poet Walt Whitman and Red Cross founder Clara Barton both served as nurses.

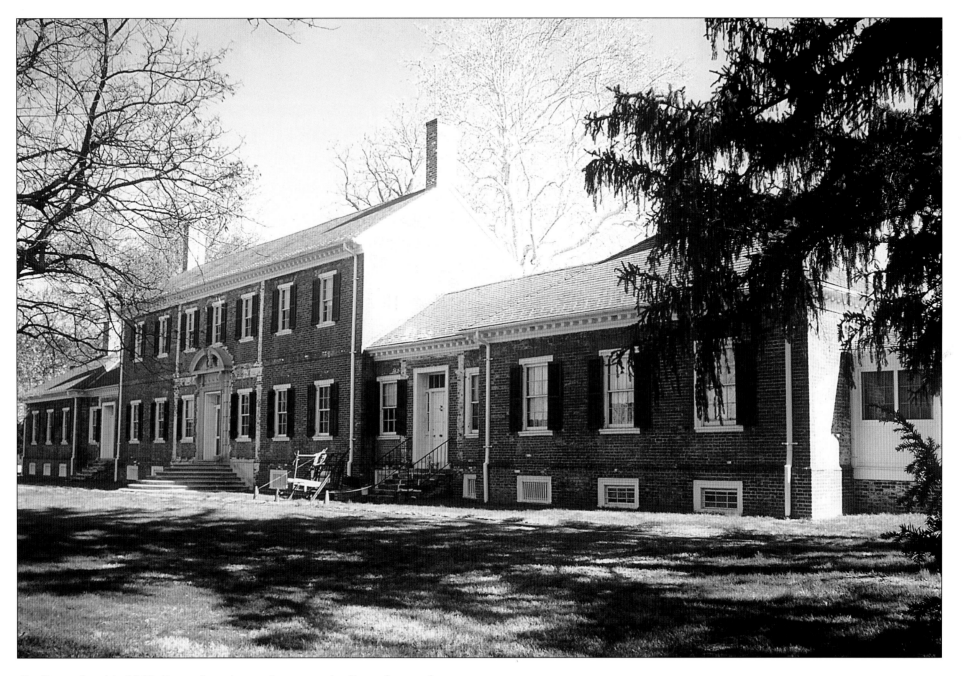

On December 11, 1862, Burnside attempted to cross the Rappahannock on pontoon bridges located just below Chatham. After the bridge builders were repeatedly fired upon by snipers on the south bank, Burnside ordered a bombardment of the town. The mansion shook from the recoil of siege guns planted on Chatham's front lawn. The house would survive the battle, as well as a second attack against Fredericksburg in May 1863, to become part of the national park in 1975.

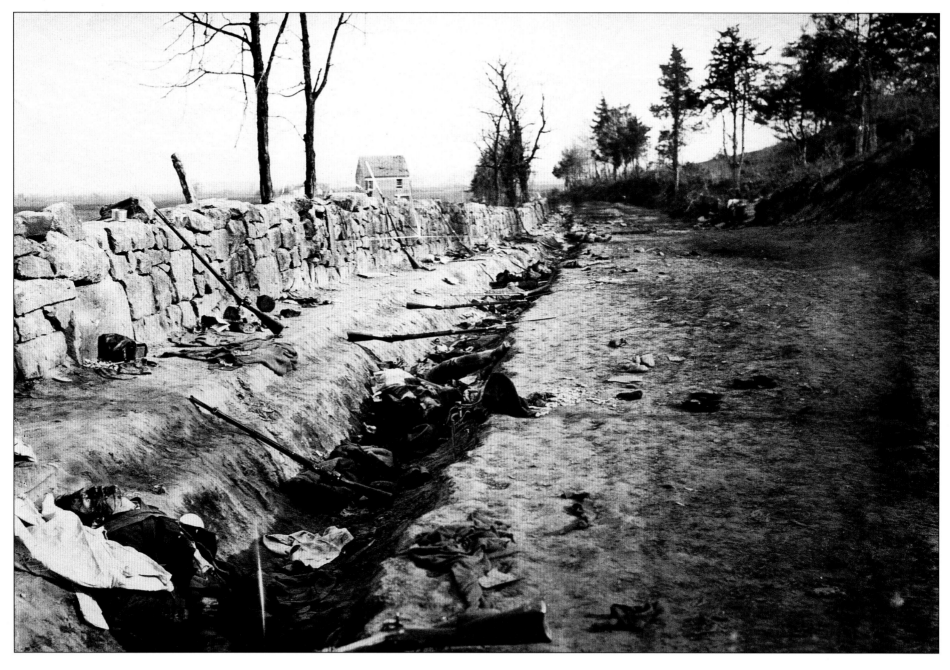

Although he had stationed sharpshooters in Fredericksburg, Lee had no intention of defending it. Instead, he placed most of his army south of the town, roughly parallel to the Richmond, Fredericksburg, and Potomac Railroad. The remainder were drawn up at the foot of Marye's Heights, in a sunken road invisible to the Union forces massing in the town. This photograph was taken in May 1863, immediately following the Second Battle of Fredericksburg.

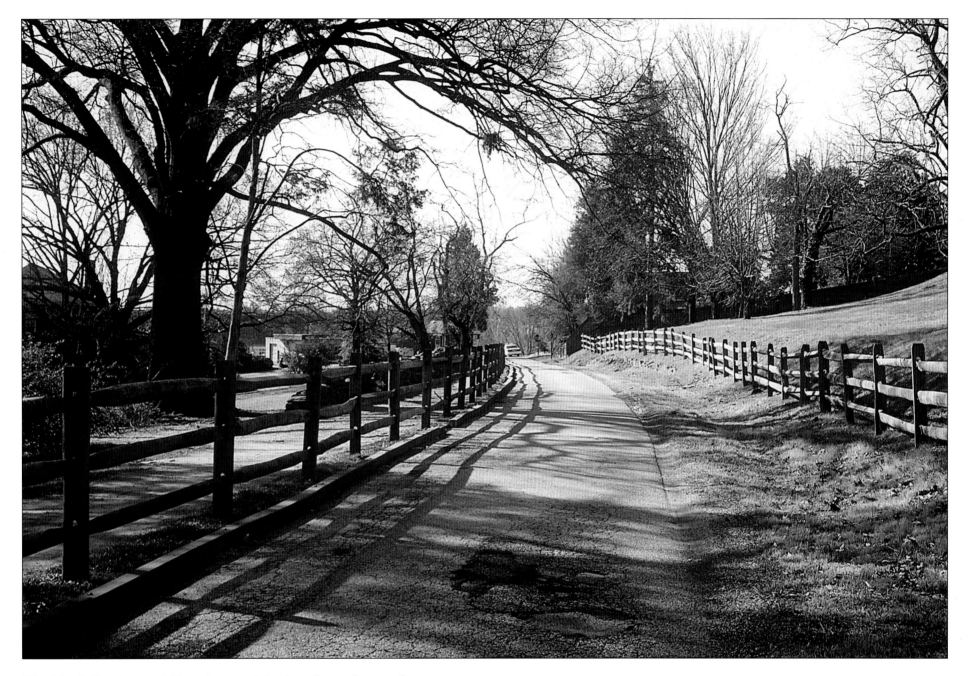

The North Carolina and Georgia men defending the sunken road on December 13, 1862, were lined up six ranks deep in some places. As the Union lines drew nearer, the gray-clad soldiers unleashed volley after volley on the unprotected bluecoats. Fifteen Union brigades made assaults against the trench, resulting in more than 8,000 Federal casualties. Today the remains of the sunken road are located beside the Fredericksburg Battlefield Visitor Center.

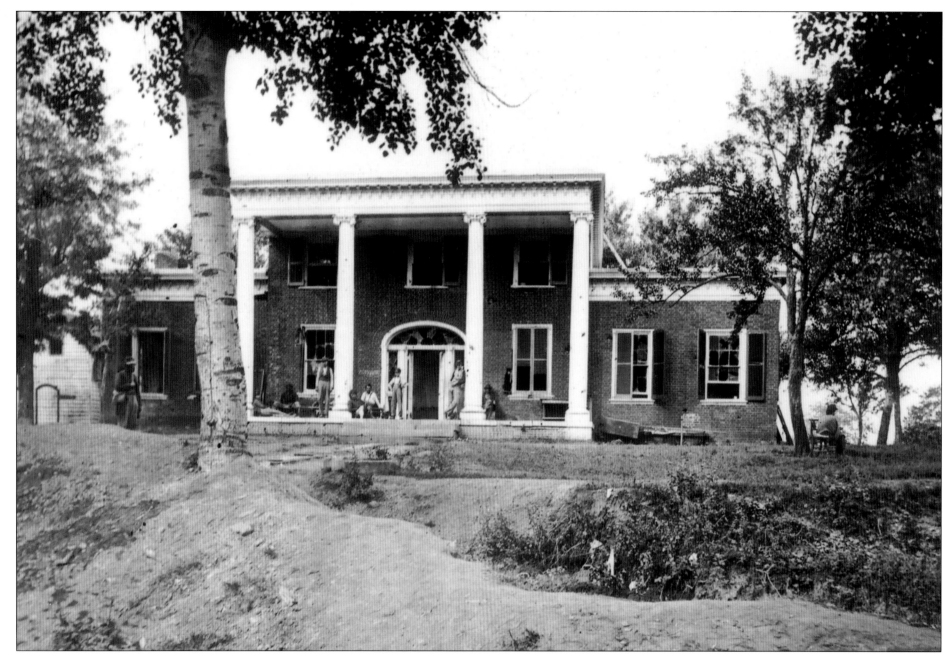

Towering behind the sunken road is Marye's Heights, named after a French Huguenot family that settled there and built Brompton, the Marye family mansion. During the battle of December 13, 1862, Marye's Heights was occupied by massed Confederate artillery. These guns blasted the waves of blue infantry attempting to seize the trench. According to one Rebel gunner, "A chicken could not live on that field when we open on it."

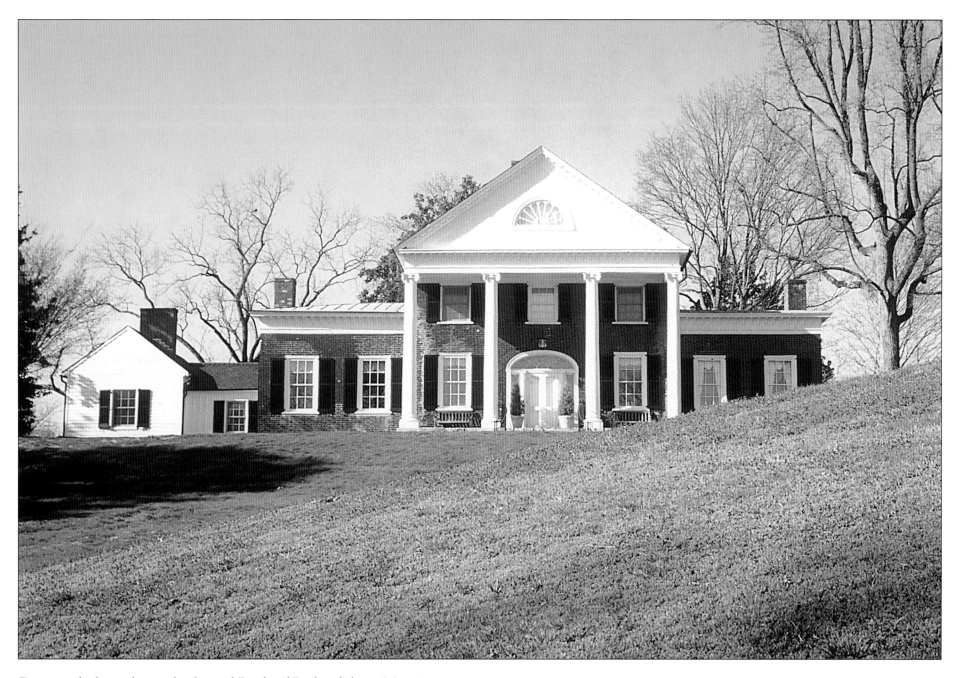

Five months later, during the Second Battle of Fredericksburg, Marye's Heights was again the key to the Confederate defense. This time, however, the Union troops were able to break the thinly held Rebel line. Today Brompton is the residence of the president of nearby Mary Washington College. South of the mansion is the Fredericksburg National Cemetery, where 16,000 Union soldiers now rest, many of them killed in the attempts to take the Heights.

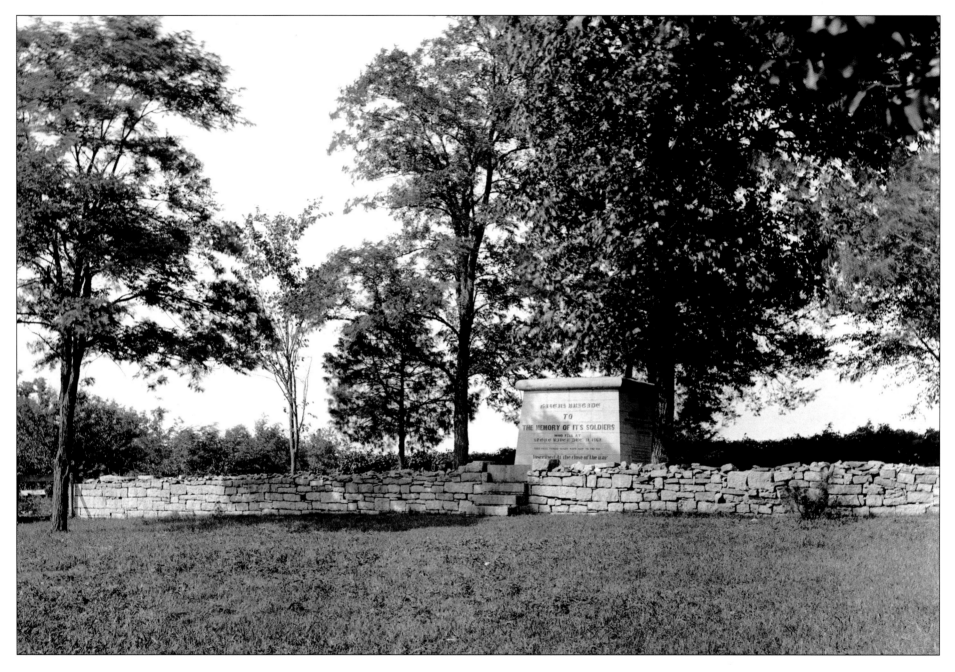

While the North was recovering from Burnside's debacle in Fredericksburg, another battle was brewing in central Tennessee. On December 31, 1862, the Confederate Army of Tennessee struck the right flank of the Union Army of the Cumberland northwest of Murfreesboro. Despite the collapse of the Union flank, the line held, thanks in part to the brave stand of Colonel William Hazen's brigade. Hazen's men held a critical portion of the Union line against four Southern assaults.

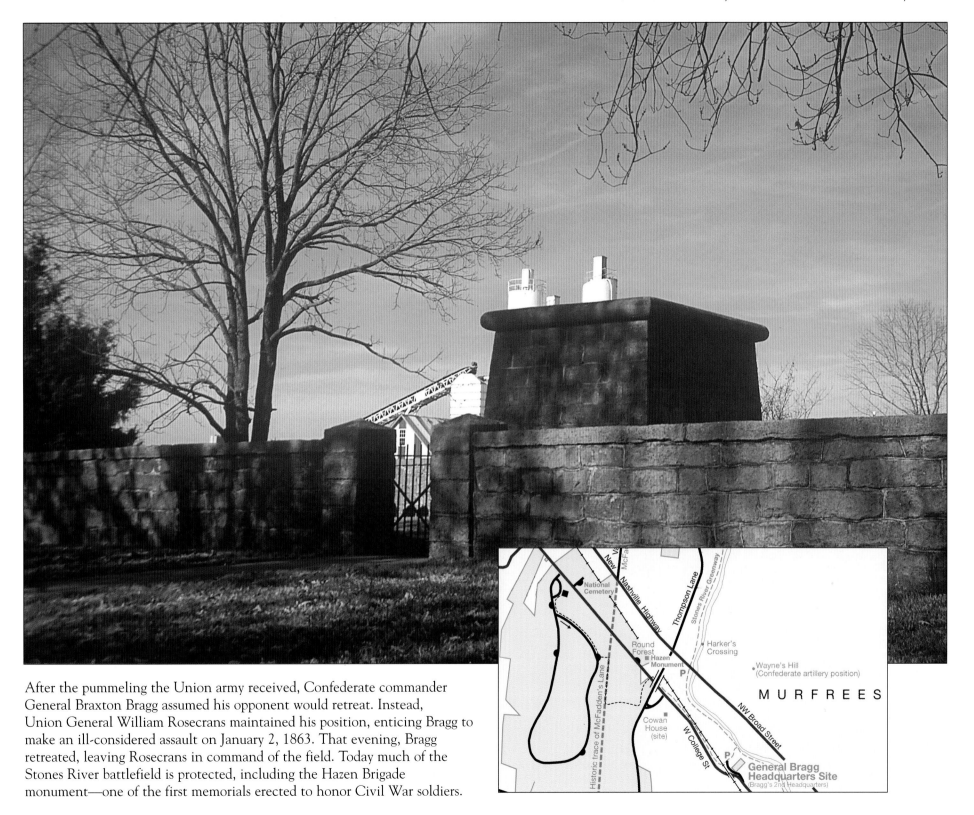

After the pummeling the Union army received, Confederate commander General Braxton Bragg assumed his opponent would retreat. Instead, Union General William Rosecrans maintained his position, enticing Bragg to make an ill-considered assault on January 2, 1863. That evening, Bragg retreated, leaving Rosecrans in command of the field. Today much of the Stones River battlefield is protected, including the Hazen Brigade monument—one of the first memorials erected to honor Civil War soldiers.

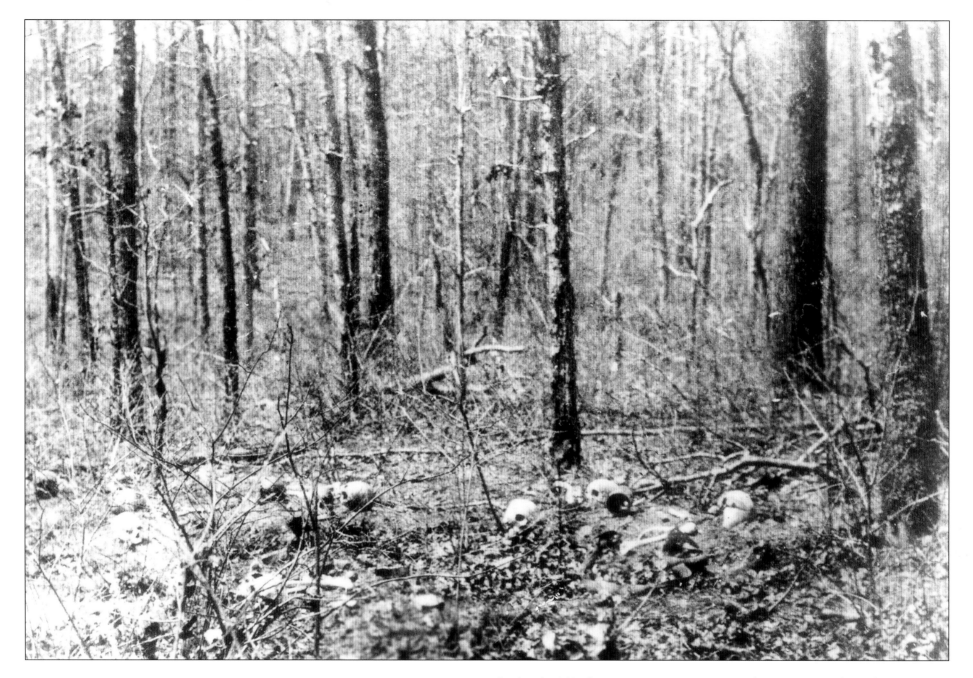

In April 1863, the nation's eyes again turned to Virginia, where the Army of the Potomac was preparing an offensive against Lee's army. The Union forces, now under the command of General Joseph Hooker, boldly swept across two rivers to reach the rear of the Confederate army. Concentrating his forces at the sleepy crossroads of Chancellorsville, Hooker felt certain he had forced Lee into a trap he could not escape.

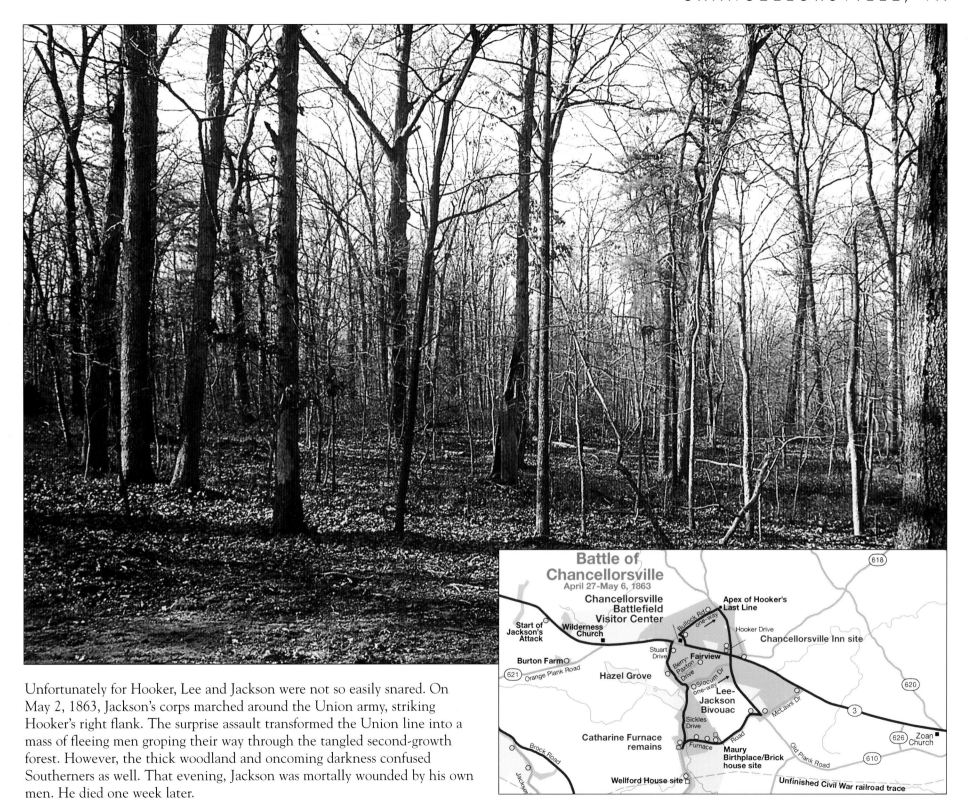

Battle of Chancellorsville
April 27–May 6, 1863

Chancellorsville Battlefield Visitor Center

Apex of Hooker's Last Line

Start of Jackson's Attack

Wilderness Church

Hooker Drive

Chancellorsville Inn site

Burton Farm

Stuart Drive

Berry-Paxton Drive

Fairview

621

Orange Plank Road

Hazel Grove

Slocum Dr one-way

Lee-Jackson Bivouac

McLaws Dr

620

3

Sickles Drive

Furnace Road

626

Zoan Church

Catharine Furnace remains

Maury Birthplace/Brick house site

Old Plank Road

610

Brock Road

Wellford House site

Unfinished Civil War railroad trace

Unfortunately for Hooker, Lee and Jackson were not so easily snared. On May 2, 1863, Jackson's corps marched around the Union army, striking Hooker's right flank. The surprise assault transformed the Union line into a mass of fleeing men groping their way through the tangled second-growth forest. However, the thick woodland and oncoming darkness confused Southerners as well. That evening, Jackson was mortally wounded by his own men. He died one week later.

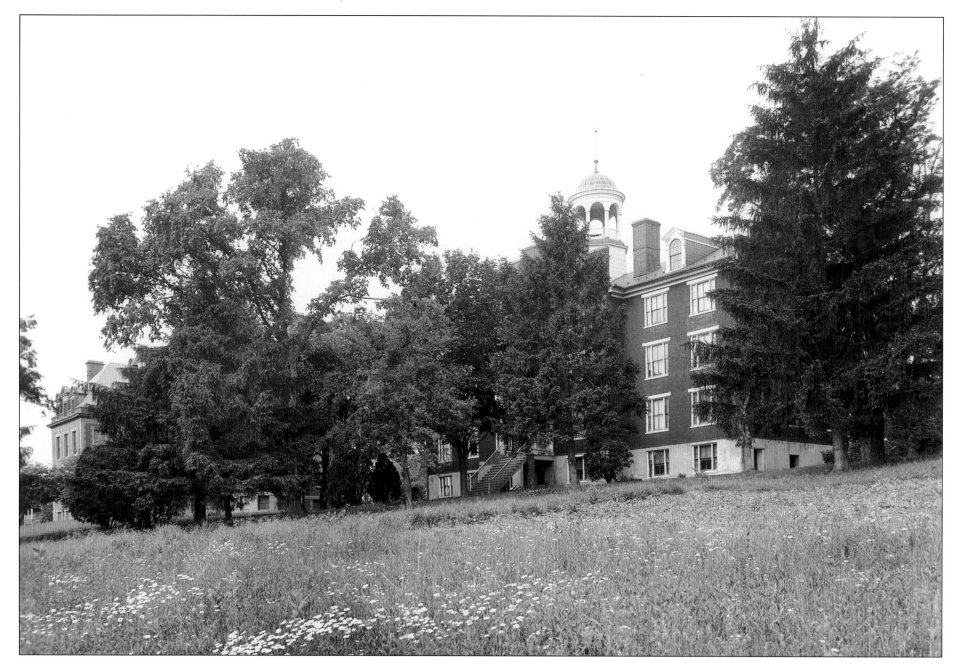

The Southern victory at Chancellorsville notwithstanding, the Confederate cause looked bleak in June 1863. Large parts of Tennessee were occupied, and the Confederacy's last bastion on the Mississippi was under siege. It fell upon Lee's army to revive Confederate fortunes. In early June, he ordered the Army of Northern Virginia toward the Potomac and Pennsylvania. On July 1, elements of his army clashed with Union cavalry on the rolling hills outside Gettysburg.

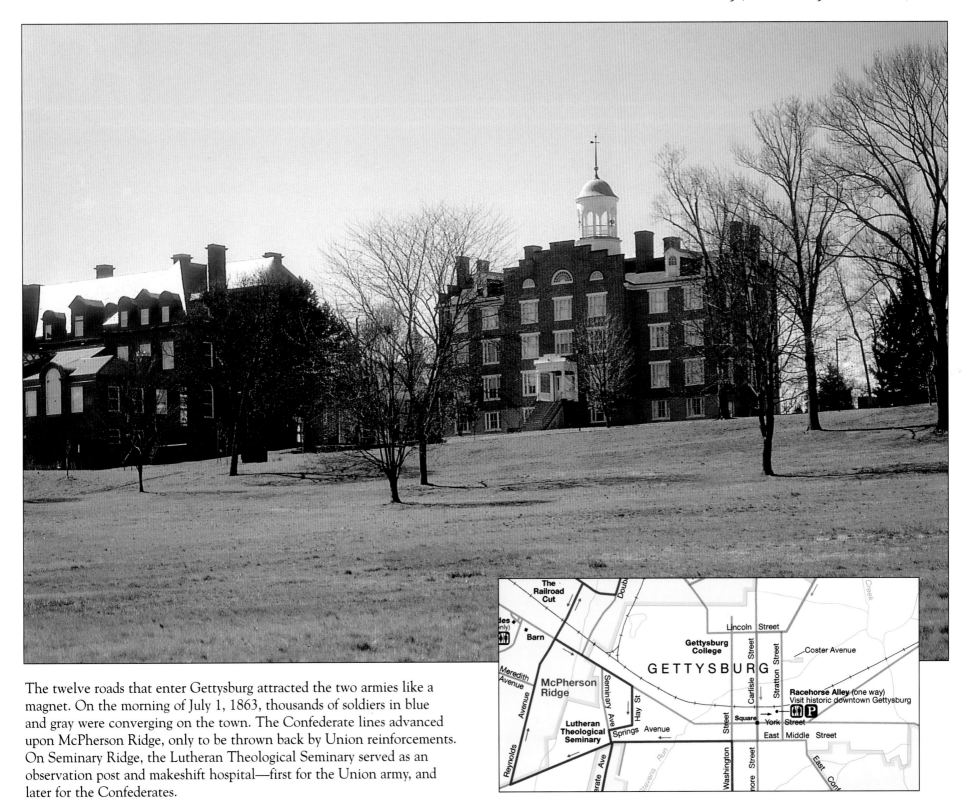

The twelve roads that enter Gettysburg attracted the two armies like a magnet. On the morning of July 1, 1863, thousands of soldiers in blue and gray were converging on the town. The Confederate lines advanced upon McPherson Ridge, only to be thrown back by Union reinforcements. On Seminary Ridge, the Lutheran Theological Seminary served as an observation post and makeshift hospital—first for the Union army, and later for the Confederates.

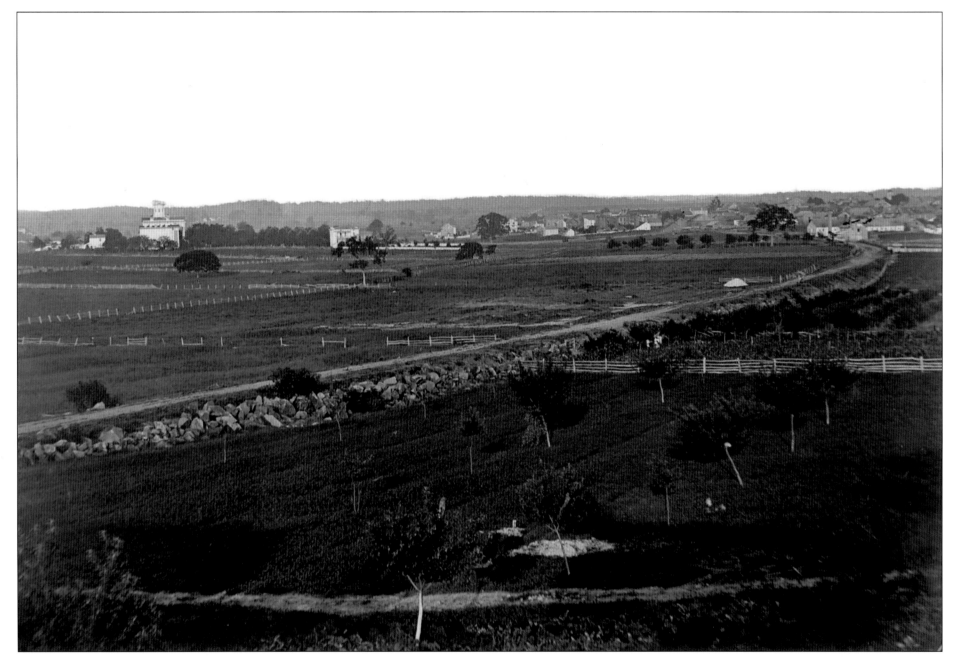

After the Confederate repulse on McPherson Ridge, a lull descended on the field as the opposing forces brought up reinforcements. On July 1, 1863, Confederate General Richard Ewell's Second Corps launched an assault north of Gettysburg that overwhelmed the thinly held Union line. After resisting the Rebels along the Harrisburg and Carlisle Pikes, the defending Union Eleventh Corps collapsed, its men fleeing into town past the imposing main hall of Pennsylvania College.

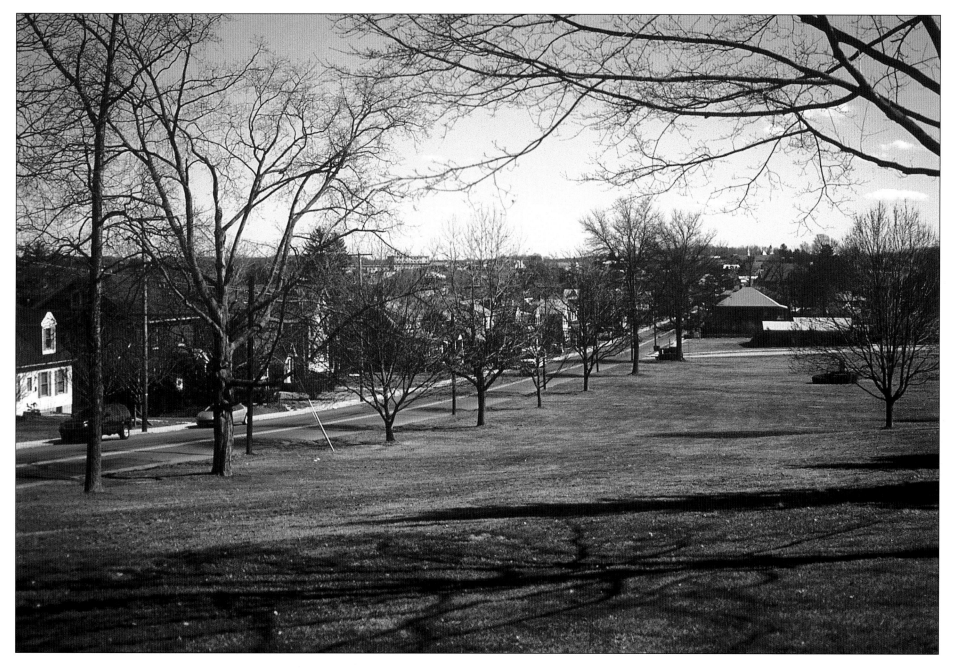

While the Eleventh Corps was struggling north of town, the Union First Corps holding Oak and McPherson Ridges was struck in both the front and flank. Like its partner to the north, the First Corps was engulfed by a gray tidal wave. The men fell back through the fields west of Gettysburg. Today those fields have all but disappeared, and the Chambersburg Pike is barely visible in the modern photograph.

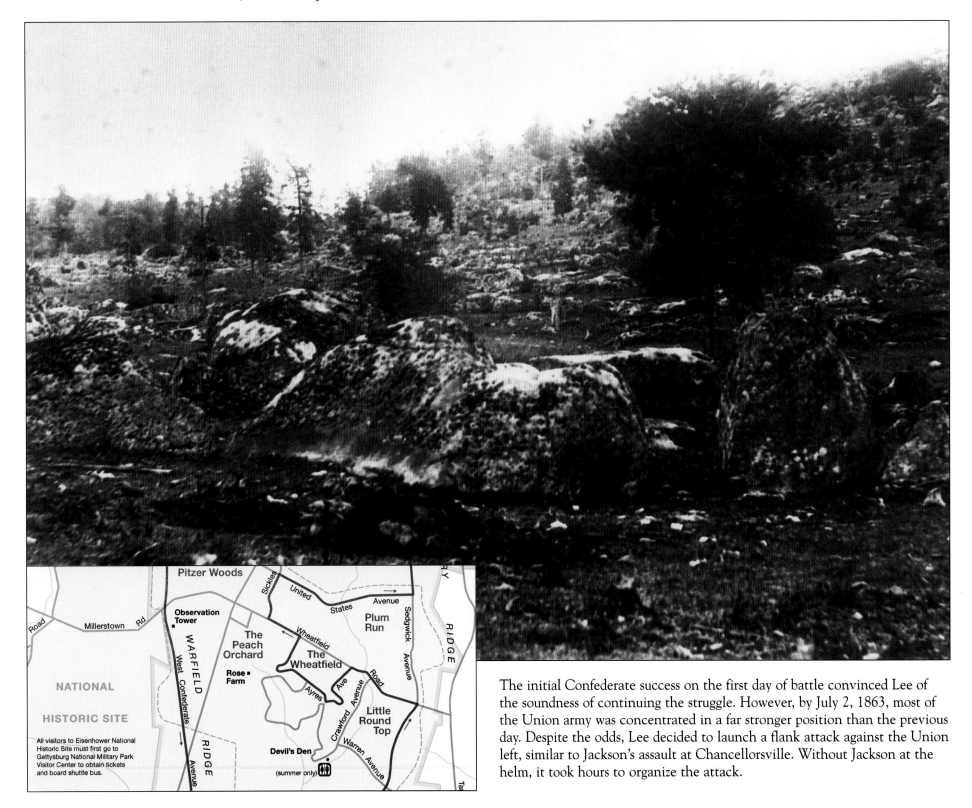

The initial Confederate success on the first day of battle convinced Lee of the soundness of continuing the struggle. However, by July 2, 1863, most of the Union army was concentrated in a far stronger position than the previous day. Despite the odds, Lee decided to launch a flank attack against the Union left, similar to Jackson's assault at Chancellorsville. Without Jackson at the helm, it took hours to organize the attack.

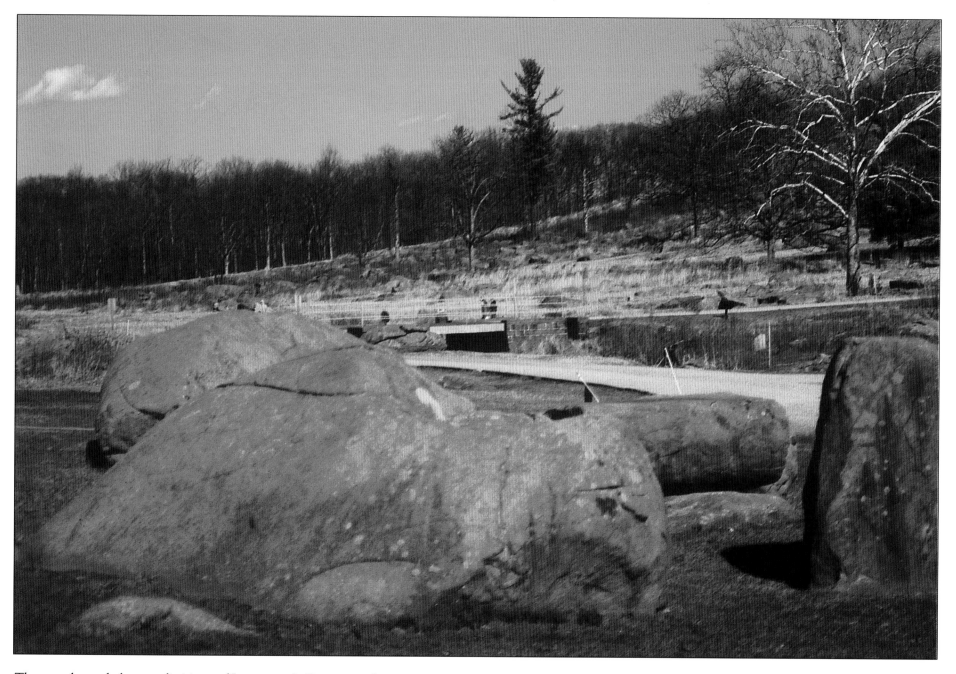

The attack, made by two divisions of Longstreet's Corps, struck an overextended Union line. Fighting swirled around Little Round Top, a key elevation on the Union flank. At the last minute, Federal reinforcements under Colonel Strong Vincent appeared on the summit, preventing the Confederates from occupying the hill. Today Little Round Top is crowned with monuments and cannons. It is also one of the most popular tourist stops on the battlefield.

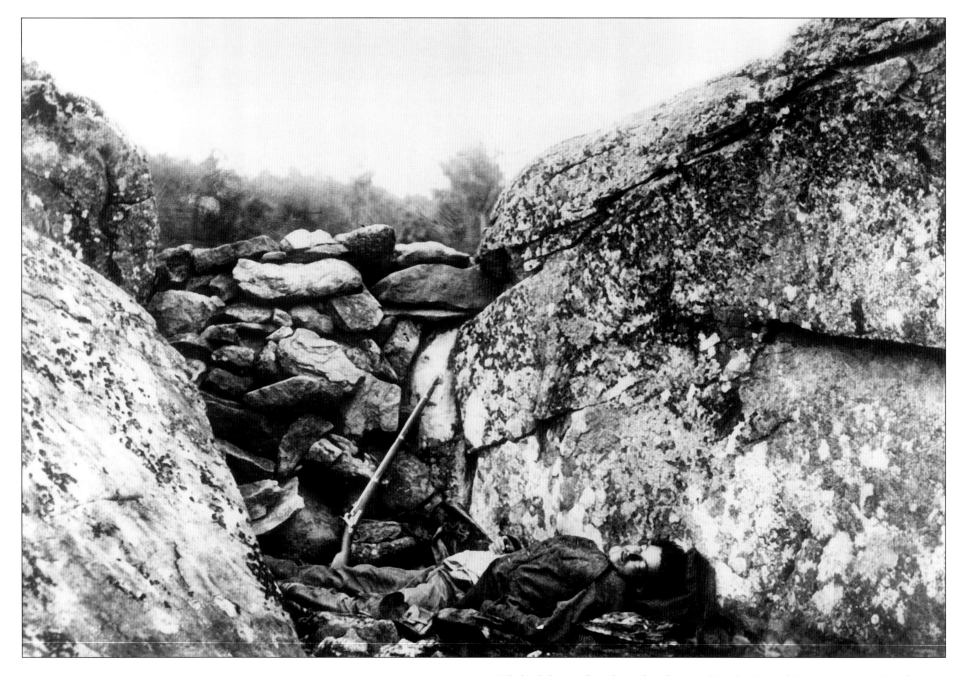

While fighting flared on the slopes of Little Round Top, Longstreet's other units sought weak spots in the Union line. One of those weak spots was Devil's Den, a jumbled cluster of huge boulders that appeared to make an excellent defensive position. However, too few Union troops were committed to holding this strategic location. Although they inflicted considerable casualties on the Confederates charging up the slope toward Devil's Den, they were unable to stop them.

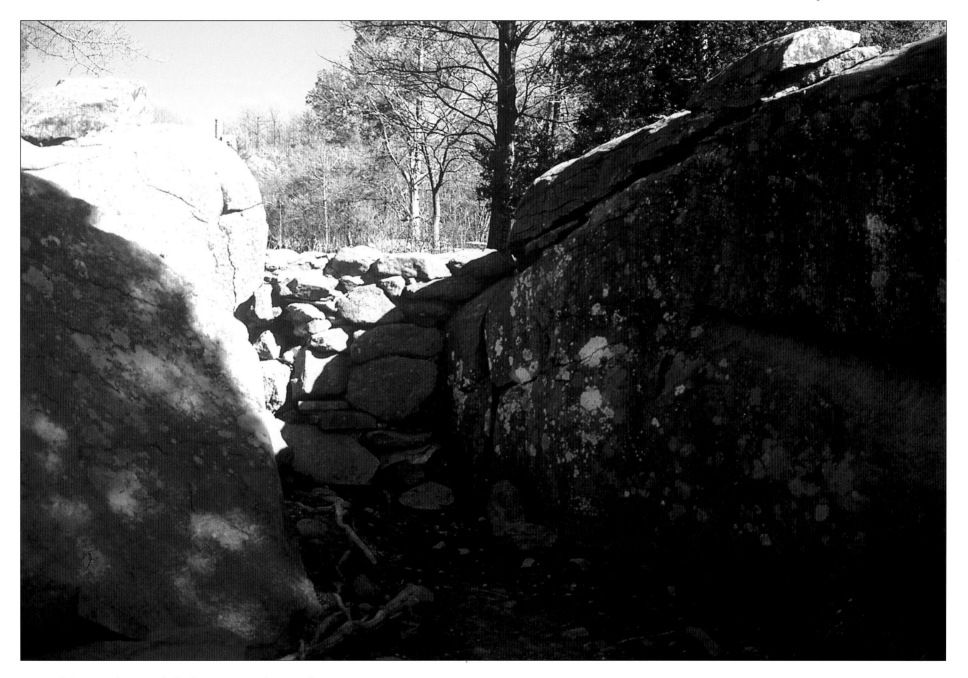

One of the Southerners killed trying to take Devil's Den was a young man shot in a nearby field. After the battle, the unburied soldier became the subject of a series of images taken by veteran photographer Alexander Gardner. Dissatisfied with the body's original location, Gardner's crew moved the corpse to an alcove within Devil's Den, later claimed by Gardner to be a sharpshooter's den. The sharpshooter's den is today preserved as part of the battlefield.

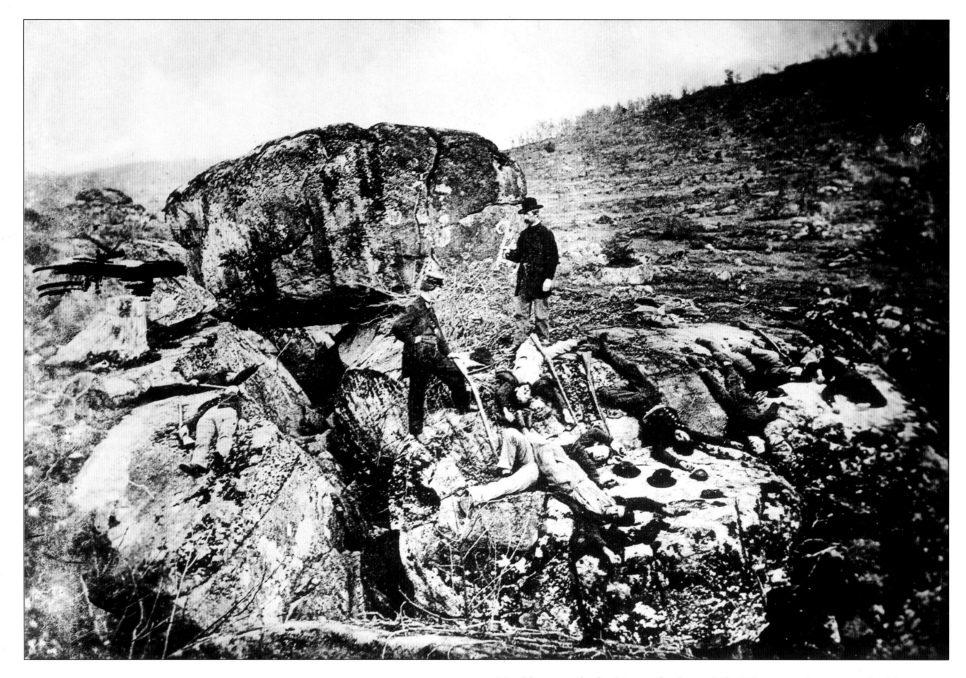

Unable to crush the Union flanks on July 2, Lee opted to storm the Union center on July 3. The attack, known as Pickett's Charge, was a spectacular failure that only added to the death toll. At the end of the three-day contest, the Gettysburg battlefield was strewn with the dead and dying. More than 50,000 men fell at Gettysburg—nearly one of every three soldiers who participated in the battle.

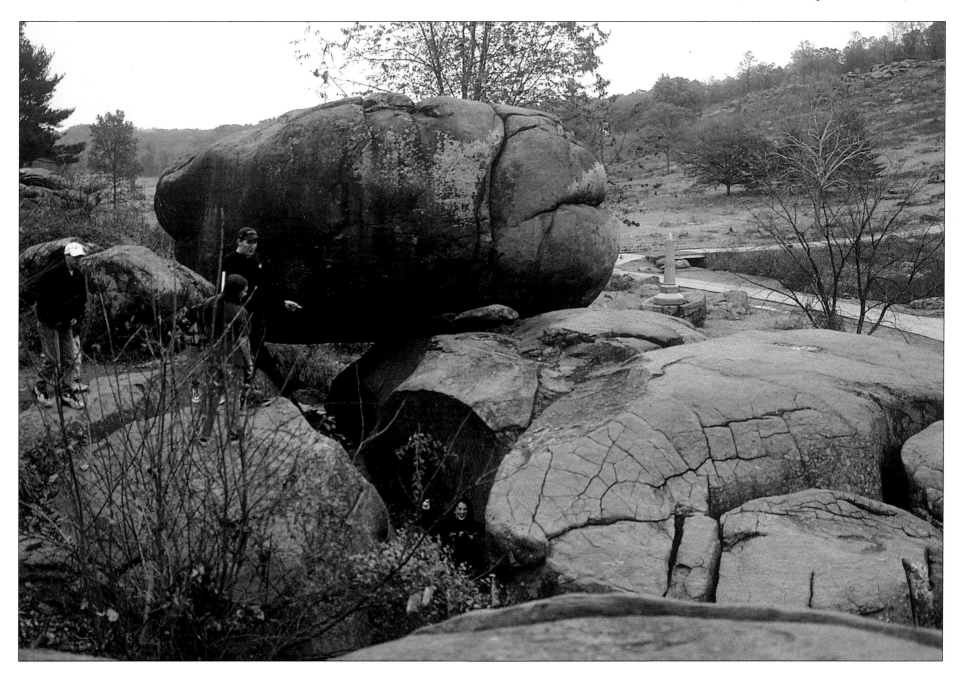

After the battle, images of Gettysburg were extremely marketable. To meet public demand, photographers flocked to Gettysburg to produce images of key battlefield landmarks. In the preceding wartime image, local photographer Peter Weaver captured Union soldiers pretending to be dead amid the rocks of Devil's Den. Today tourists tramp among the boulders where soldiers once fought and later posed for the camera.

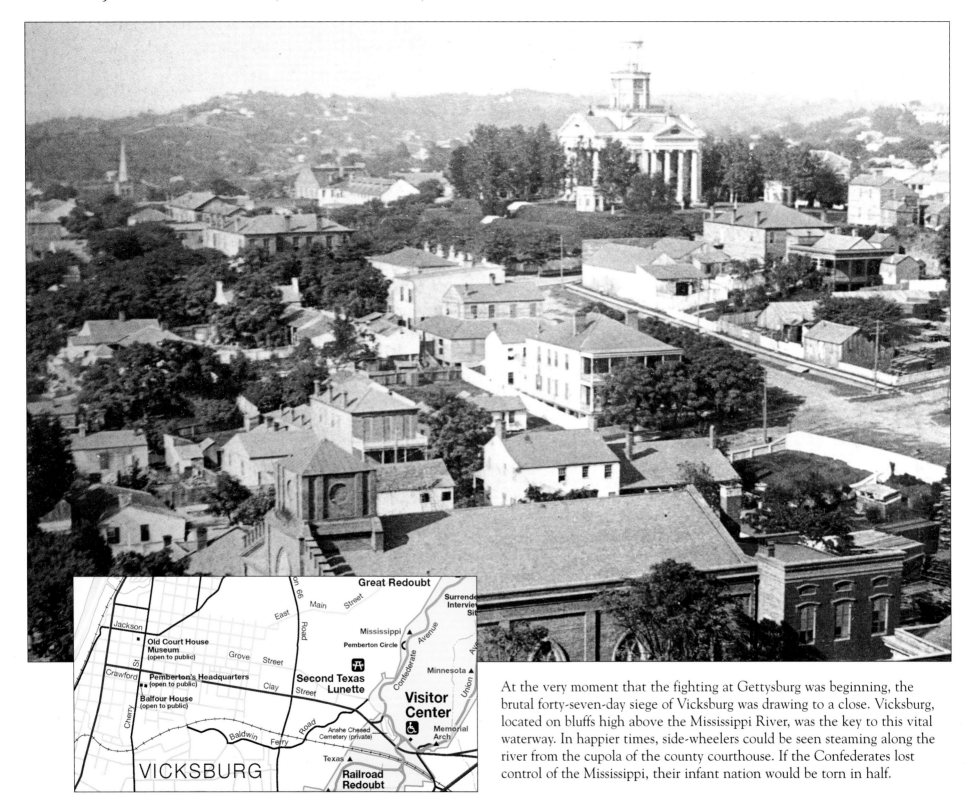

At the very moment that the fighting at Gettysburg was beginning, the brutal forty-seven-day siege of Vicksburg was drawing to a close. Vicksburg, located on bluffs high above the Mississippi River, was the key to this vital waterway. In happier times, side-wheelers could be seen steaming along the river from the cupola of the county courthouse. If the Confederates lost control of the Mississippi, their infant nation would be torn in half.

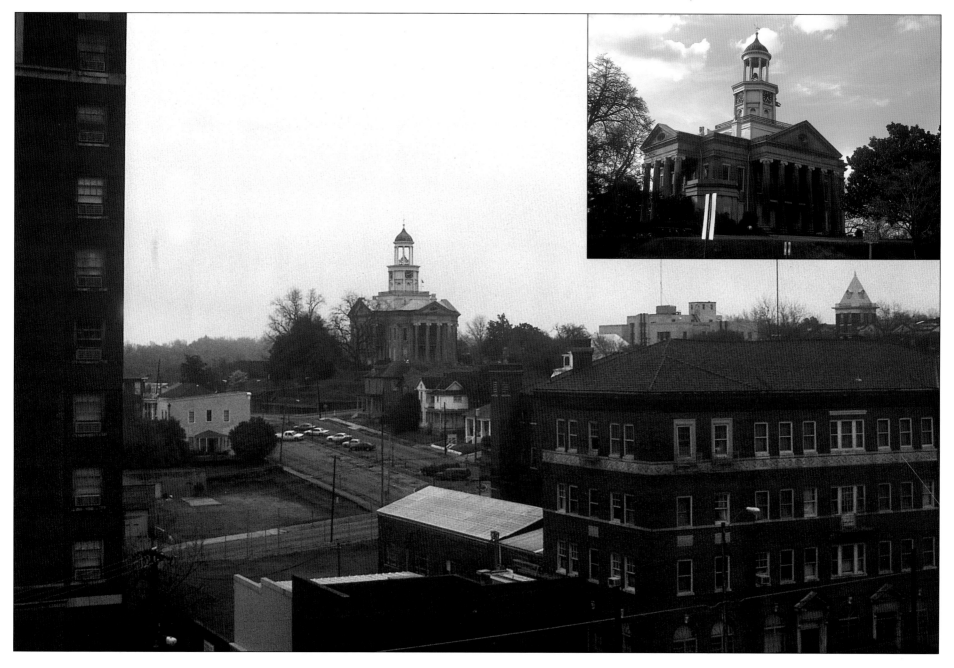

Lincoln, a Kentuckian by birth and an Illinoisan by adoption, grew up traveling on the flatboats that traversed the Mississippi and its tributaries. He too recognized the enormous strategic importance of Vicksburg. In November 1861, Lincoln remarked to a group of Union officers, "Vicksburg is the key. The war can never be brought to a close until that key is in our pocket."

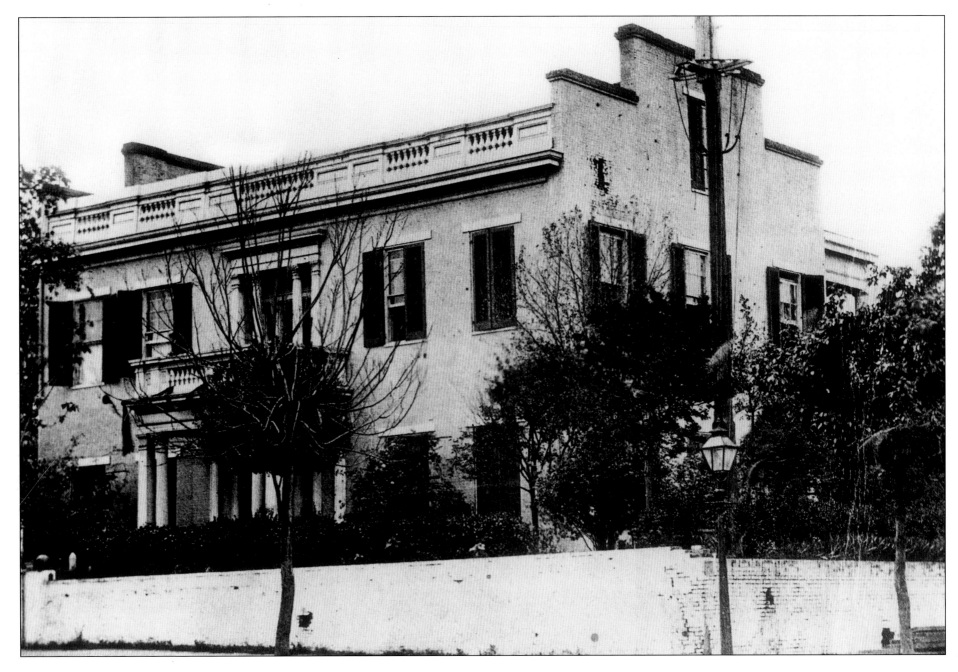

The job of taking Vicksburg fell on the stooped shoulders of Union General Ulysses S. Grant. Grant, a failure in both the peacetime army and private life, was gaining a reputation as a pugnacious fighter. Despite being surprised at Shiloh, he had risen to command the principal Union army in the West. Given the enormous obstacles facing the Federal army, perhaps no other Union general was better suited for the daunting task.

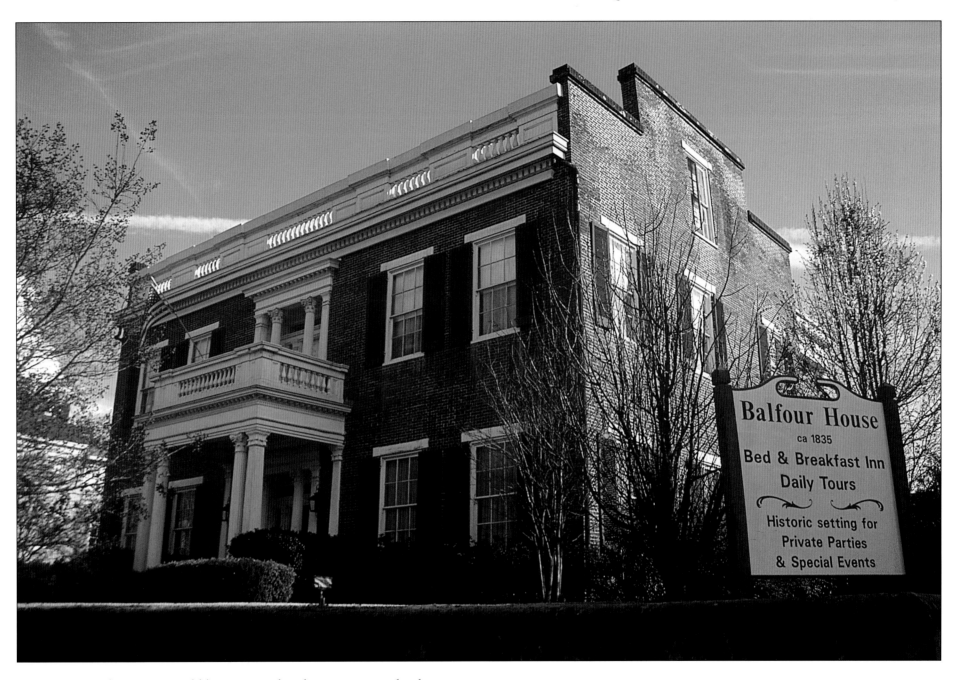

For seven months, Grant would be consumed with attempts to take the city. In late 1862, he began an unsuccessful overland campaign against Vicksburg. Grant was forced to retreat and his chief lieutenant, General William T. Sherman, was repulsed at Chickasaw Bayou. Undaunted, Grant determined to renew the contest in the spring. His untiring efforts would eventually meet with success, and he would stay in this house in occupied Vicksburg, now a bed and breakfast.

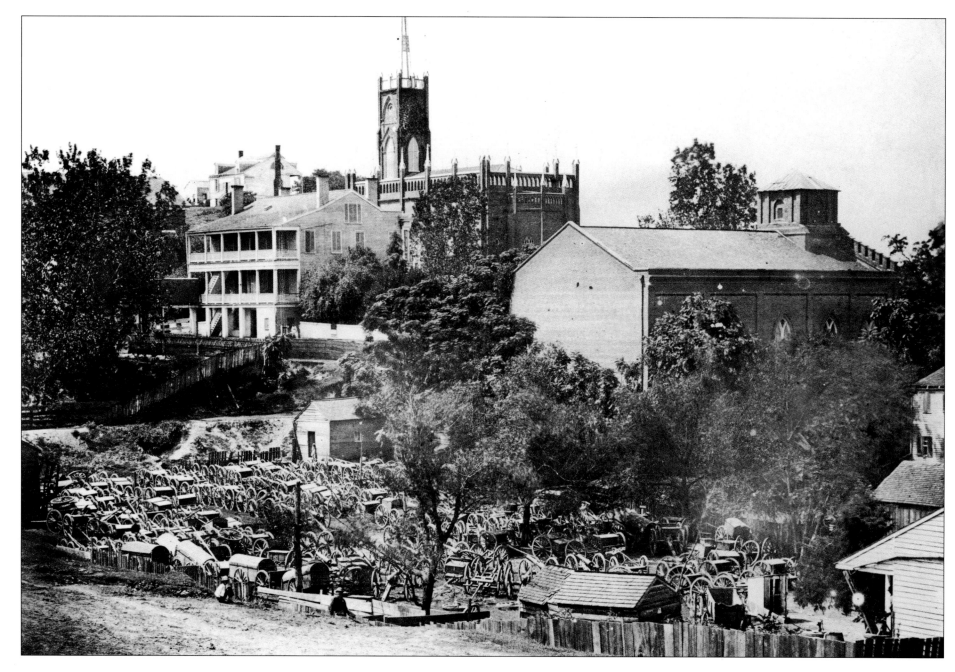

Grant had to devise a way to come to grips with the army defending Vicksburg. In late April 1863, Grant's army embarked on one of the most brilliant campaigns of the war. He ordered his men to march down the west bank of the Mississippi and cross the great river south of Vicksburg. In a series of running battles, Grant captured the state capital at Jackson and forced the Confederates back into the defenses of Vicksburg.

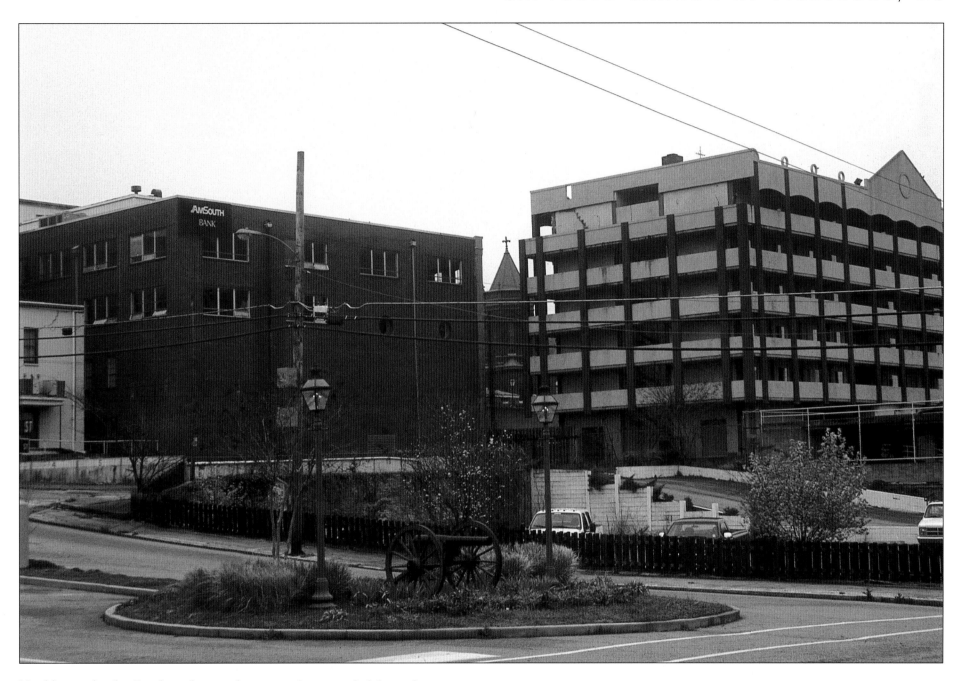

Unable to take the Southern bastion by storm, Grant settled down for a
siege. For the Confederates defending the city, Vicksburg was a death trap.
Unable to escape, they slowly starved. On July 4, 1863, after the siege, the
Rebels capitulated, surrendering enormous amounts of small arms and
cannons. Today it is hard to imagine the hundreds of captured ordnance
wagons that once sat in the shadow of Vicksburg's churches.

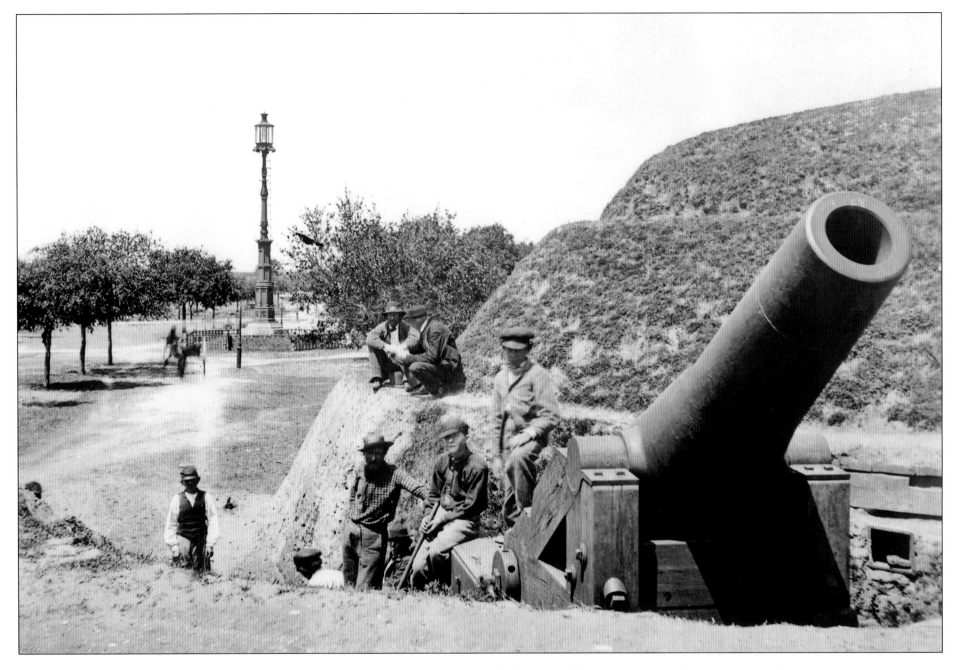

To the east of Vicksburg, Union forces were equally determined to take Charleston, a key Southern port and symbol of Confederate resistance. In April 1863, a fleet of Yankee ironclad warships under the command of Rear Admiral Samuel Du Pont attempted to storm past Fort Sumter and break into Charleston Harbor. However, the Rebel defenders, ably led by General P. G. T. Beauregard, easily repulsed the dreaded iron monsters, sinking one of them.

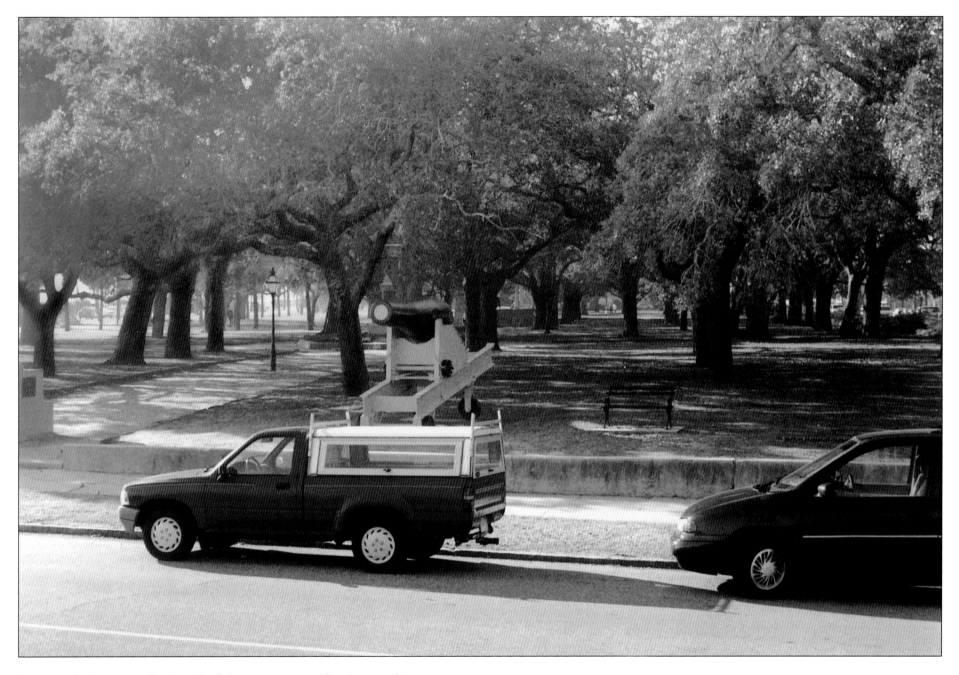

In spite of their triumph, the Confederates were not leaving anything
to chance. In the event that the Union ironclads were ever able to
penetrate the harbor, Charlestonians had prepared a powerful reception
committee. In the once-peaceful setting of White Point Gardens, they
planted four of the heaviest guns in the South, including a twelve-inch
Blakely cannon manufactured in England. Clearly, Charleston would
not surrender without a fight.

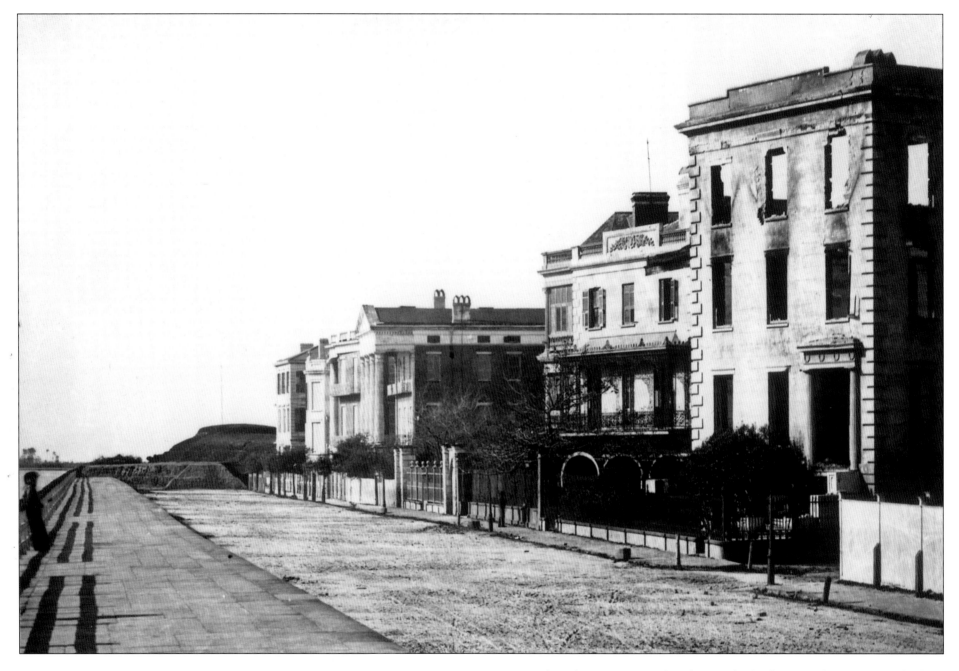

Frustrated in their attempt to break into the harbor, Northerners launched a combined army-navy expedition against Morris Island in July 1863. The northern tip of the island, located just yards from Fort Sumter, was defended by two bastions known as Batteries Wagner and Gregg. Despite several Union attacks, including a gallant assault by the African-American troops of the 54th Massachusetts Infantry, the two forts held out until September 7.

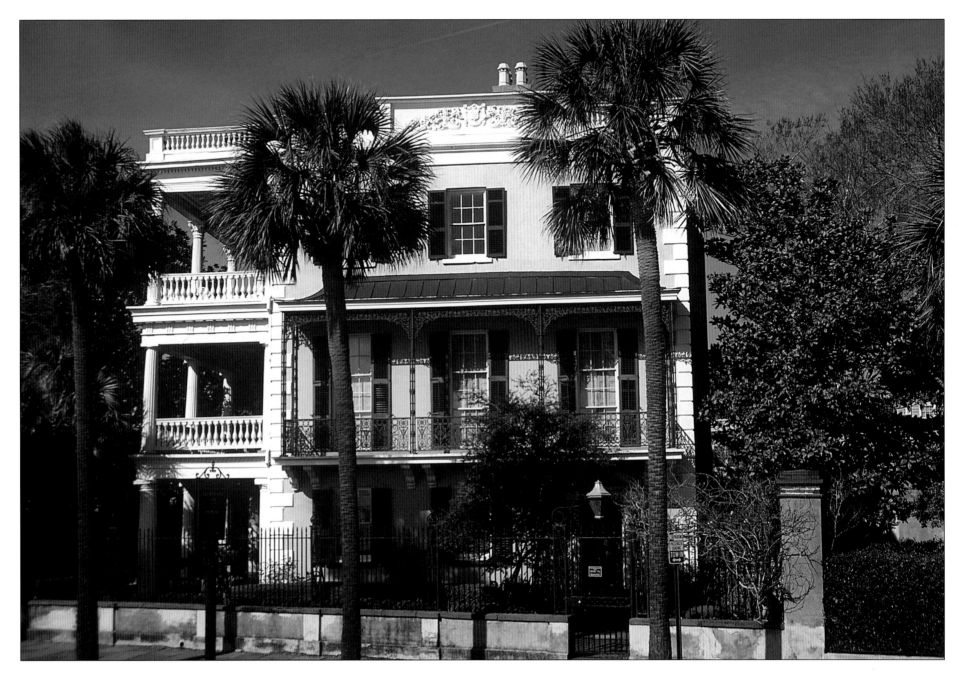

The Union occupation of Morris Island, as well as parts of nearby James Island, enabled vengeful Federal gunners to target Charleston itself. Nearly the entire city was within range of the Union cannons. Particularly hard hit were the picturesque mansions along East Battery Street. Although the shell-torn and fire-gutted Heyward House has long since been torn down, its neighbor, the Edmonston-Alston mansion, has been preserved by the Middleton Place Foundation.

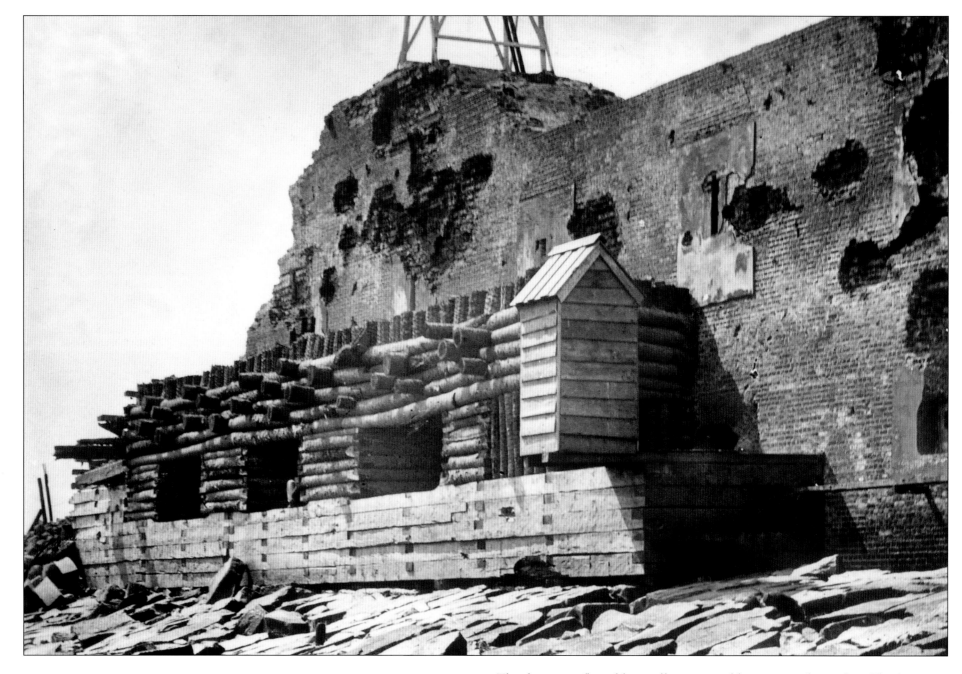

The damage inflicted by artillerymen in blue was not limited to Charleston. Quincy Gilmore, the hero of Fort Pulaski, was in command of the Union cannoneers on Morris Island. Gilmore was convinced he could destroy Sumter with a barrage launched from the island. Even before the fall of Batteries Wagner and Gregg, Gilmore had begun a sustained bombardment of Sumter. The Confederates used palmetto logs to make crude repairs to the battered fort.

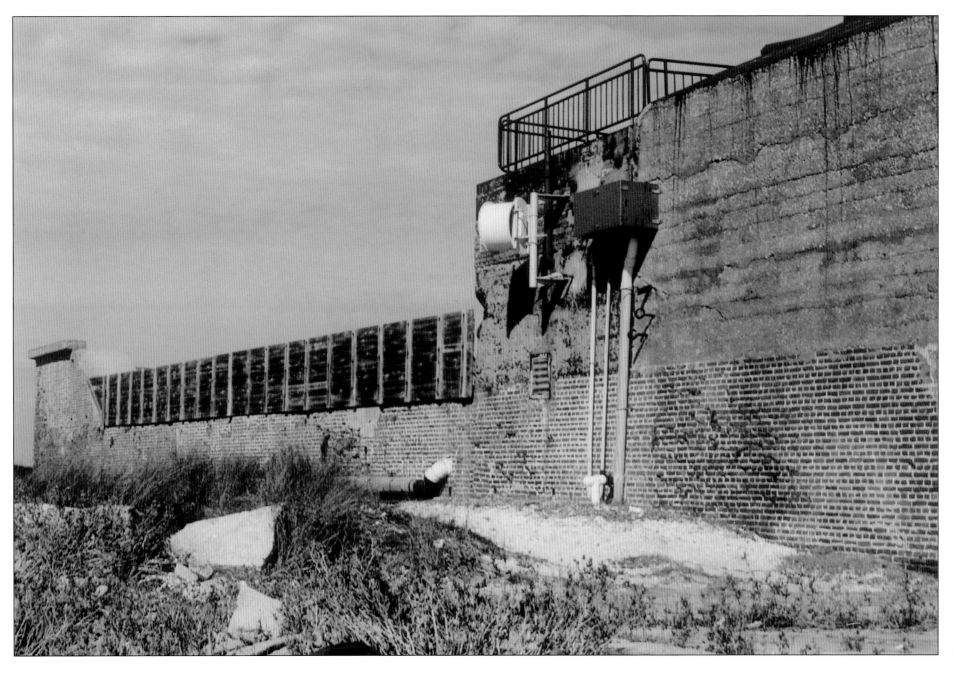

Makeshift repairs could not compensate for the damage wreaked by the constant pounding of the heavy guns. The walls were pulverized into rubble, transforming the citadel into a powerful earthwork. Although most of the fort's cannons were dismounted by the sustained bombardment, the Confederates continued to maintain a substantial presence at Sumter. On the night of September 8, 1863, the Sumter garrison repulsed a Union storming party intent on capturing the fort.

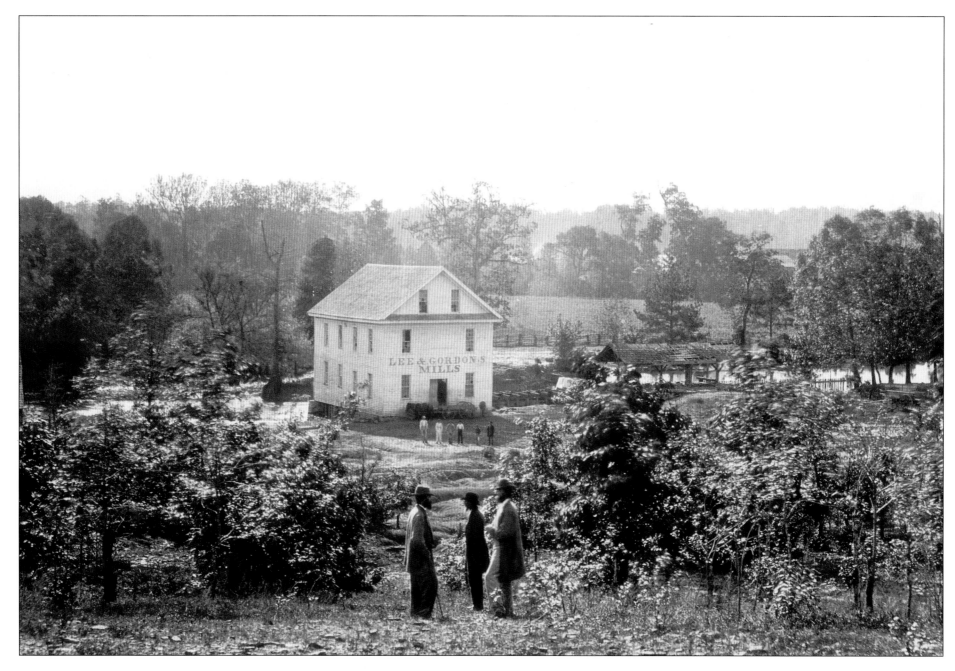

The defeats at Vicksburg and Gettysburg had cast a pall over the Confederacy. The only hope for restoring Southern fortunes seemed to be a concentration of Rebel forces in northern Georgia. On September 19, 1863, Confederate General Bragg threw his reinforced legions across Chickamauga Creek in Georgia in an effort to crush the Union Army of the Cumberland. One of the few landmarks in the vicinity was Lee and Gordon's Mills, located on the southern extremity of the battlefield.

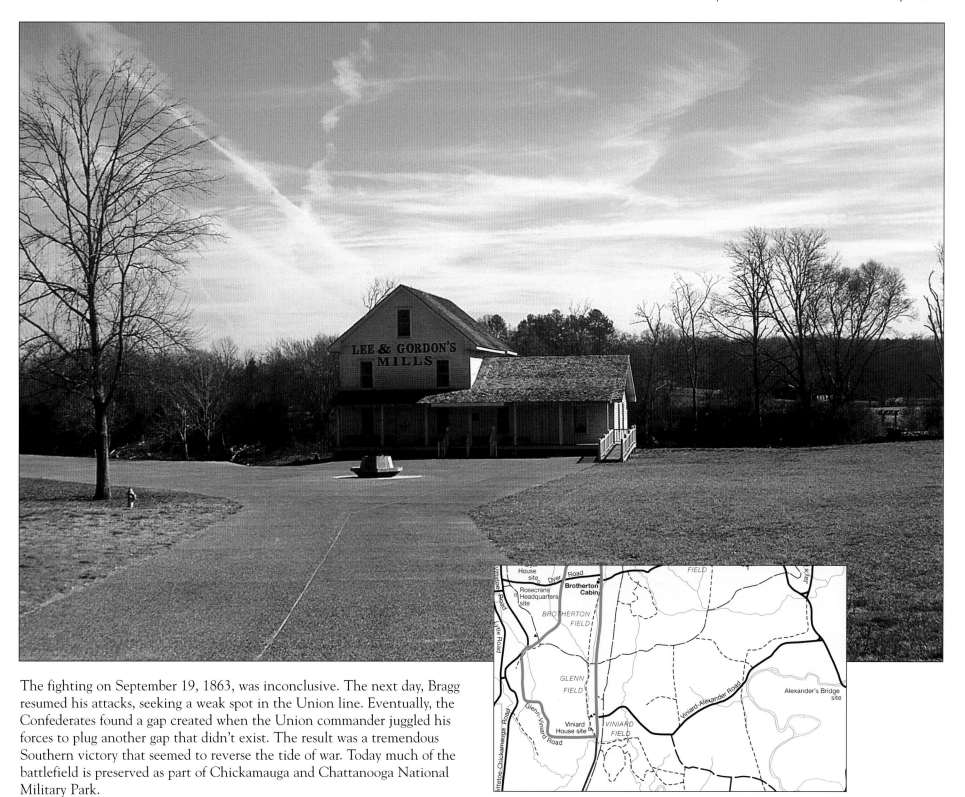

The fighting on September 19, 1863, was inconclusive. The next day, Bragg resumed his attacks, seeking a weak spot in the Union line. Eventually, the Confederates found a gap created when the Union commander juggled his forces to plug another gap that didn't exist. The result was a tremendous Southern victory that seemed to reverse the tide of war. Today much of the battlefield is preserved as part of Chickamauga and Chattanooga National Military Park.

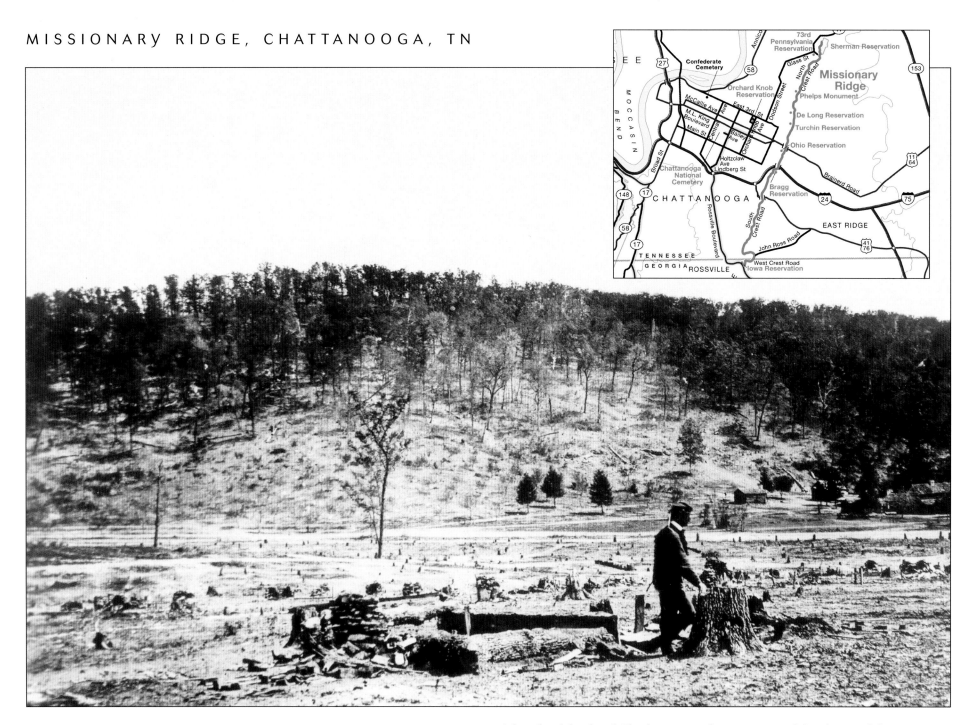

After the debacle of Chickamauga, the survivors of the Army of the Cumberland streamed back to their supply base at Chattanooga. The Yankee army, battered and dispirited, was in dire straits. Only Bragg's lackluster pursuit, combined with Union General George H. Thomas's heroic stand on Snodgrass Hill, prevented the Chickamauga defeat from becoming a disaster. On September 23, 1863, Bragg lay siege to Chattanooga by seizing control of Missionary Ridge.

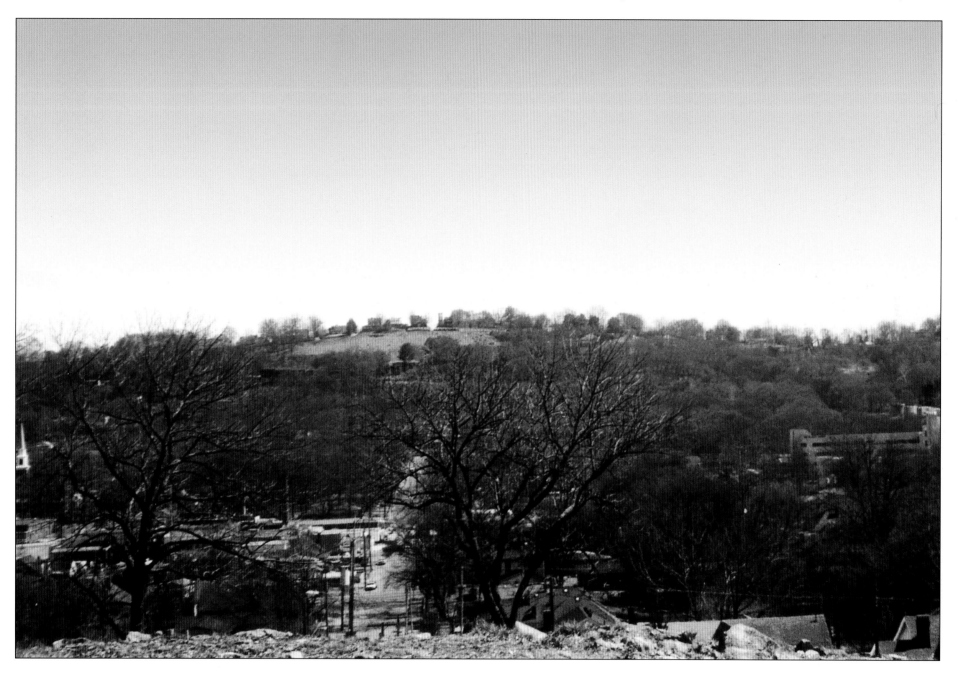

For two months, the Army of the Cumberland sat in besieged Chattanooga, surviving on reduced rations and awaiting succor from Union armies under Generals Grant and Hooker. Grant was given overall command of the forces around Chattanooga, with the understanding that his immediate objective was the defeat of Bragg. In late October 1863, he opened the "cracker line" to supply the Cumberland Army and on November 24 he launched his attack against Bragg.

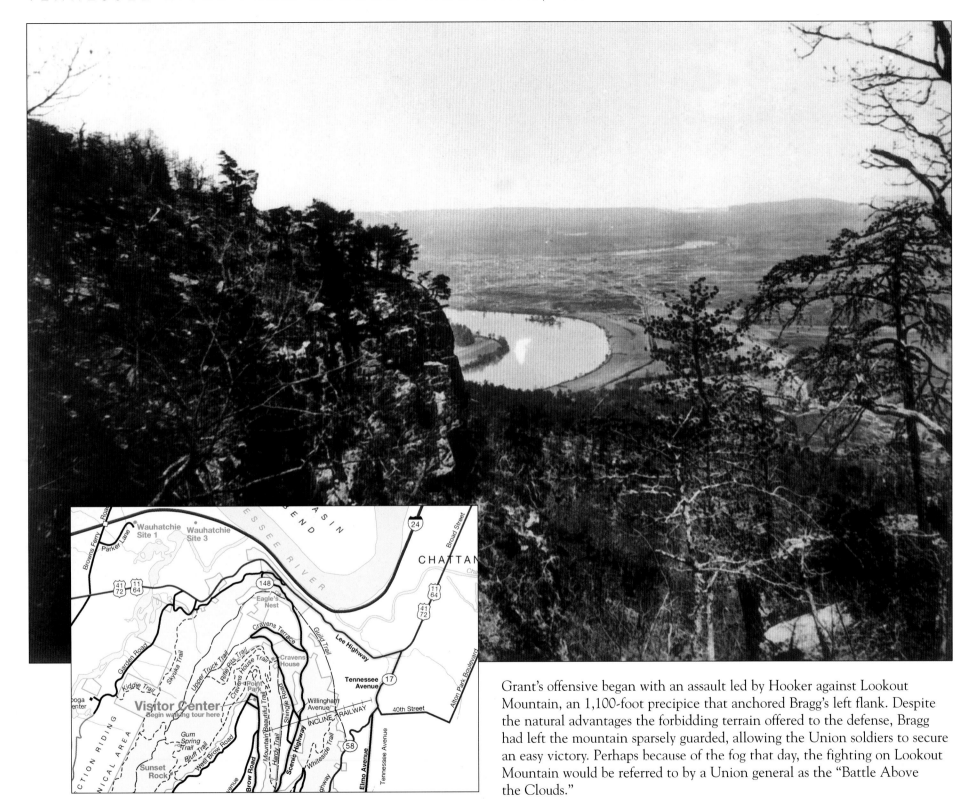

Grant's offensive began with an assault led by Hooker against Lookout Mountain, an 1,100-foot precipice that anchored Bragg's left flank. Despite the natural advantages the forbidding terrain offered to the defense, Bragg had left the mountain sparsely guarded, allowing the Union soldiers to secure an easy victory. Perhaps because of the fog that day, the fighting on Lookout Mountain would be referred to by a Union general as the "Battle Above the Clouds."

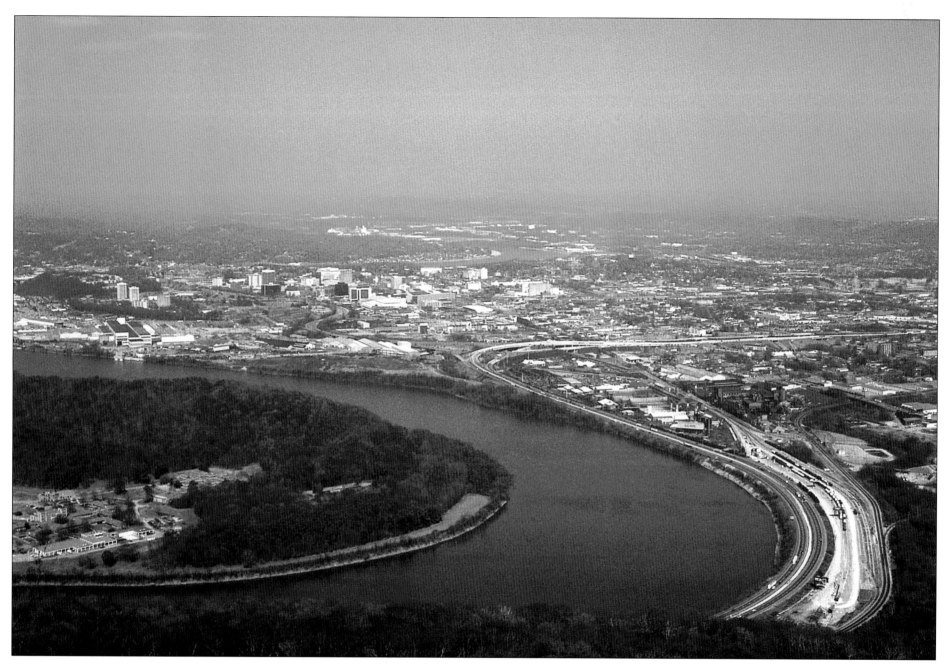

The next day, Grant sent General Sherman against Bragg's right flank, hoping that Sherman could force the evacuation of Missionary Ridge. However, Sherman was stalled by Confederate General Patrick Cleburne's skillful defense of Tunnel Hill. It then fell upon the Army of the Cumberland to attack Missionary Ridge in an assault that routed the Rebels in a manner reminiscent of the Union rout at Chickamauga two months before.

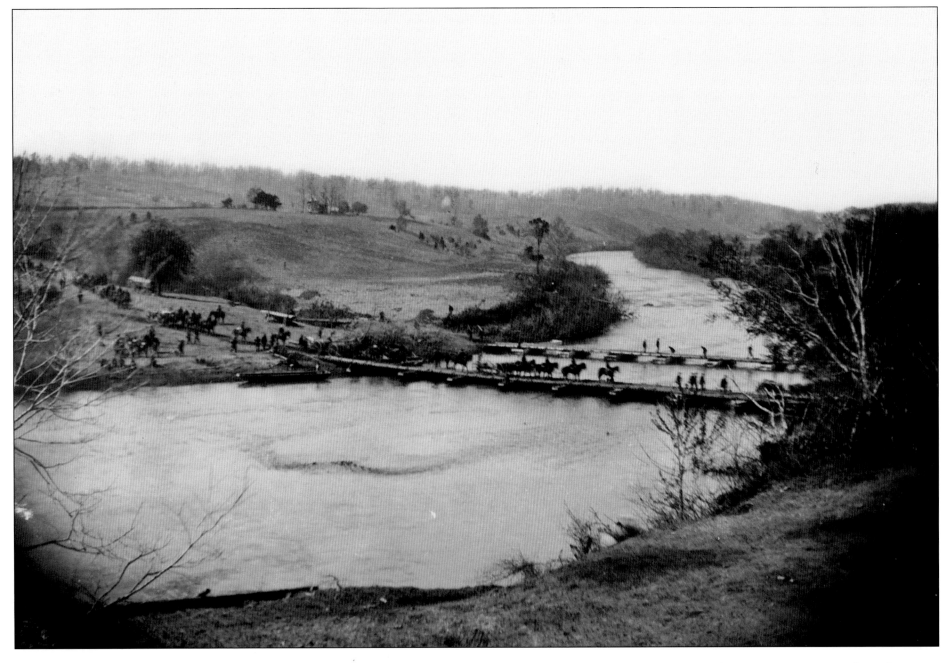

Due in large measure to his victory at Chattanooga, Grant was brought east in March 1864 to take command of all the Union armies. Rather than sit behind a desk in Washington, Grant chose to make his headquarters with the ill-fated Army of the Potomac. In May, he led that army southward, across the Rapidan River at Germanna Ford, and into the Wilderness where the Confederate army of Robert E. Lee was waiting.

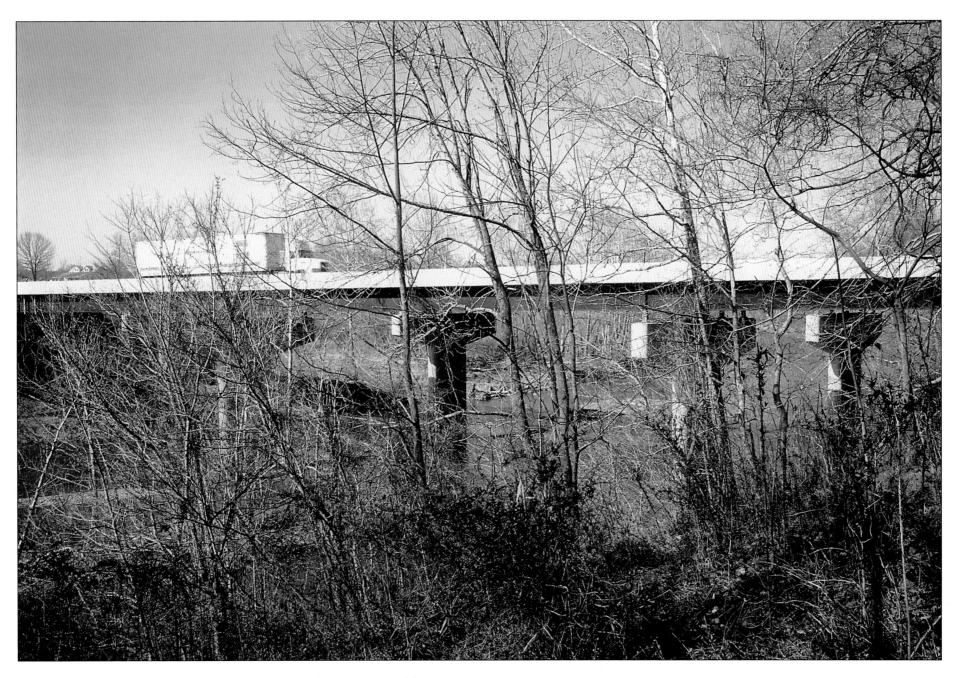

The two-day Battle of the Wilderness pitted more than 160,000 soldiers
in gray and blue against one another in one of the bloodiest struggles
of the Civil War. Fought in the thickets and secondary growth forest of
Spotsylvania County, the battle was a series of clashes for control of the
few roads in the vicinity. The result was a tactical draw, but Grant's refusal
to retreat back across the Rapidan gave him a moral victory.

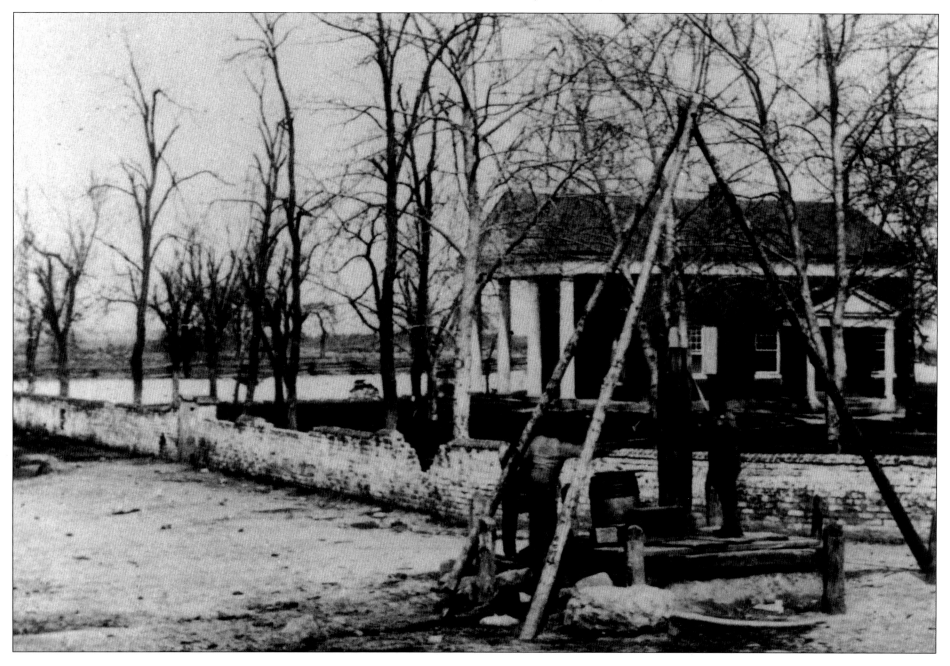

After the Wilderness, the armies raced for the crossroads town of
Spotsylvania, located on the main road to Richmond. Lee
won the race, but by the slimmest of margins. His dismounted cavalry
held off the Union army just long enough for the Confederate infantry
to arrive. At the time of the battle, Spotsylvania itself was little more than
a cluster of buildings and the courthouse shown in this period image.

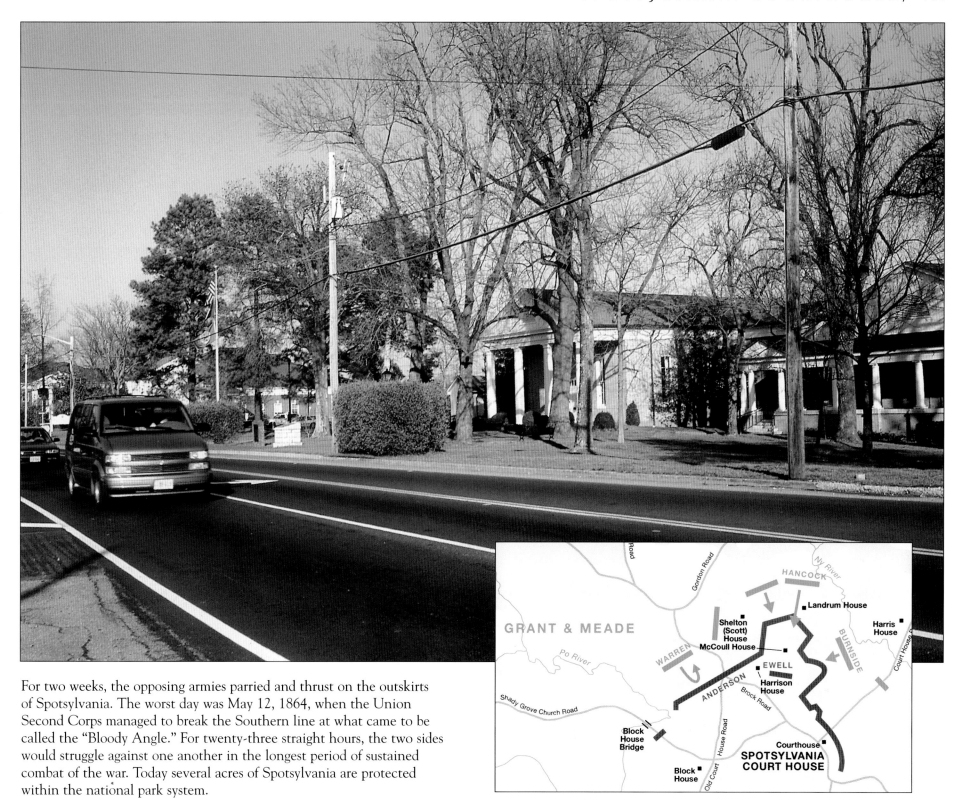

For two weeks, the opposing armies parried and thrust on the outskirts of Spotsylvania. The worst day was May 12, 1864, when the Union Second Corps managed to break the Southern line at what came to be called the "Bloody Angle." For twenty-three straight hours, the two sides would struggle against one another in the longest period of sustained combat of the war. Today several acres of Spotsylvania are protected within the national park system.

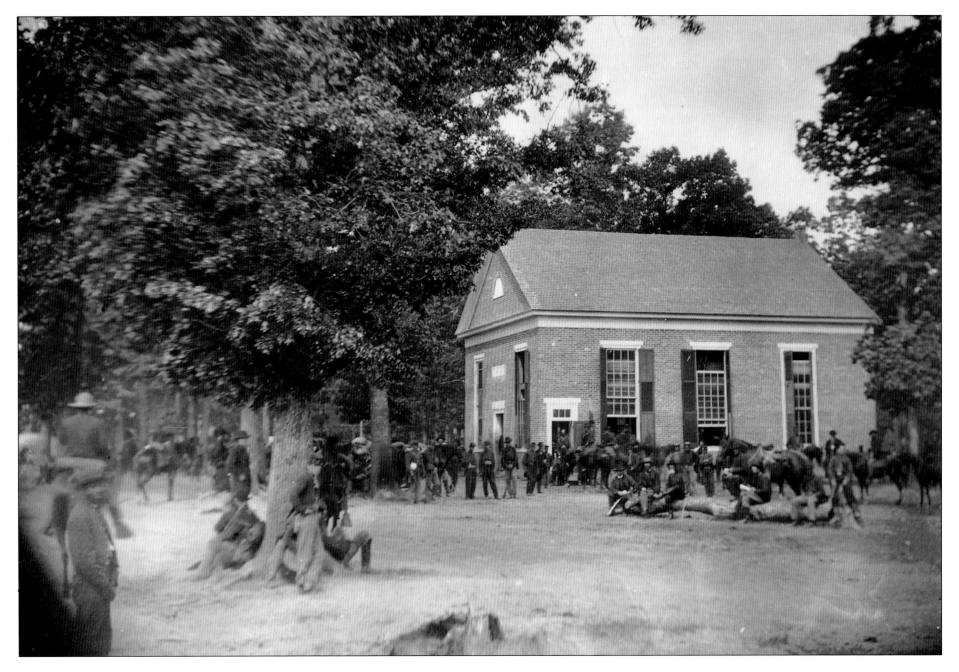

That evening, Lee withdrew from the Bloody Angle, taking up a shorter line just south of the scene of the fight on May 12, 1864. The carnage of the Bloody Angle left many nearly speechless. According to a Massachusetts soldier, "I cannot begin to tell you the horrors I have seen…the Rebels are piled up in heaps three or four deep and the pit is filled with them piled up dead and wounded."

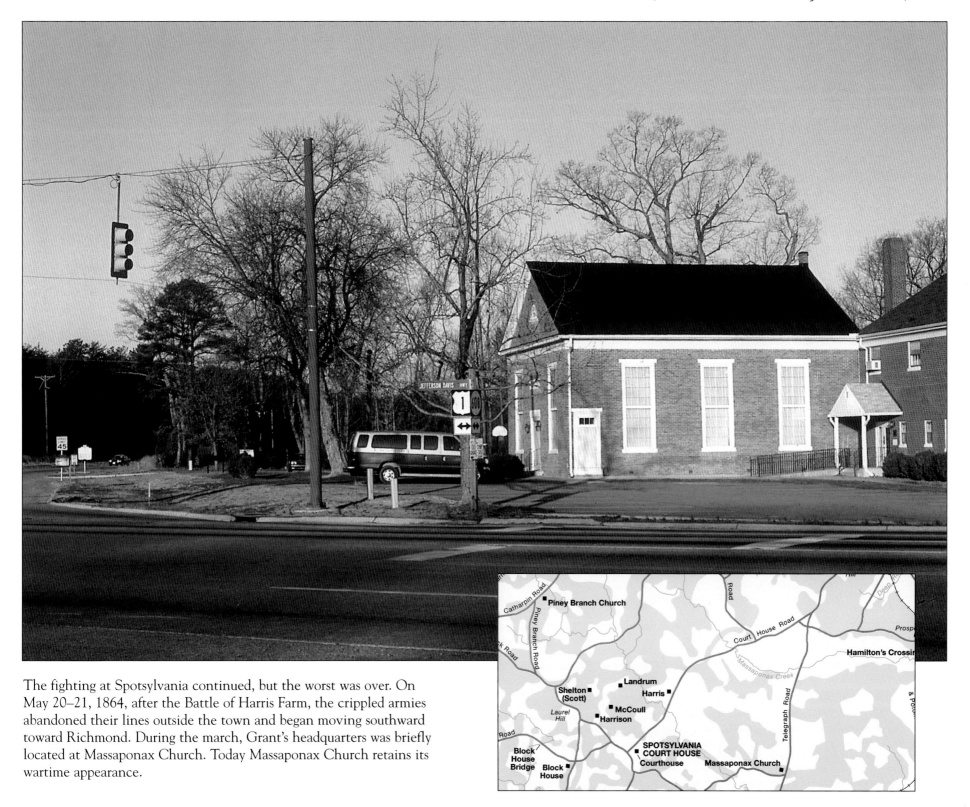

The fighting at Spotsylvania continued, but the worst was over. On May 20–21, 1864, after the Battle of Harris Farm, the crippled armies abandoned their lines outside the town and began moving southward toward Richmond. During the march, Grant's headquarters was briefly located at Massaponax Church. Today Massaponax Church retains its wartime appearance.

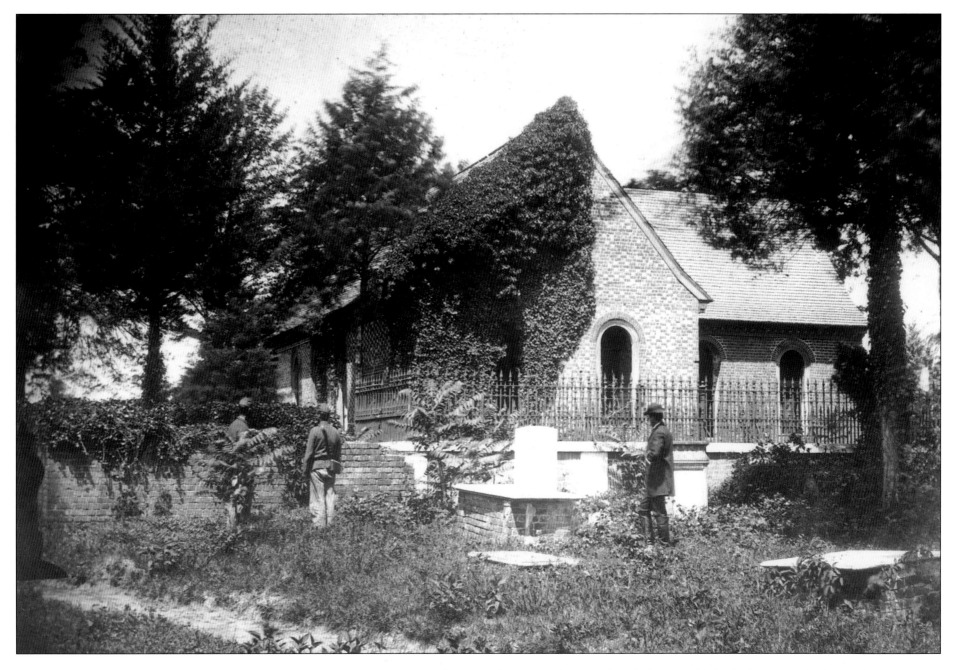

Throughout May and early June 1864, Lee's Army of Northern Virginia would continue to parry Grant's attempt to leapfrog between the Confederate army and Richmond. The armies clashed at North Anna, Totopotomoy Creek, and Cold Harbor, in the process lengthening already unprecedented casualty lists. Finally, Grant concluded that victory lay not in front of Richmond, but to the south, at the vital railroad center of Petersburg.

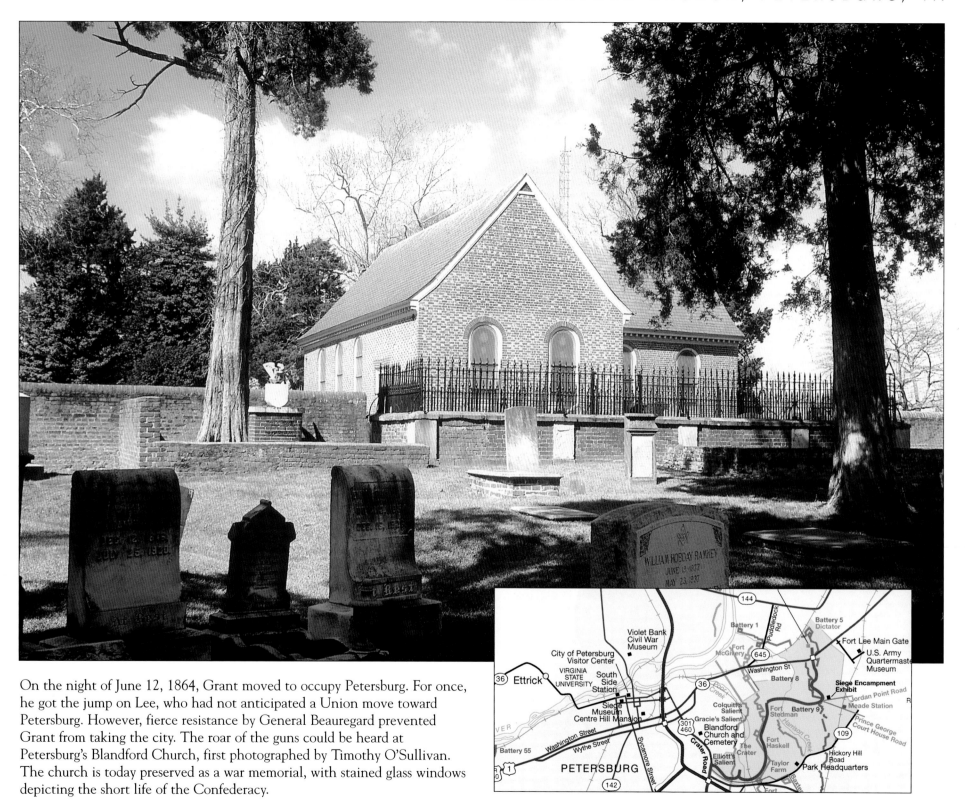

On the night of June 12, 1864, Grant moved to occupy Petersburg. For once, he got the jump on Lee, who had not anticipated a Union move toward Petersburg. However, fierce resistance by General Beauregard prevented Grant from taking the city. The roar of the guns could be heard at Petersburg's Blandford Church, first photographed by Timothy O'Sullivan. The church is today preserved as a war memorial, with stained glass windows depicting the short life of the Confederacy.

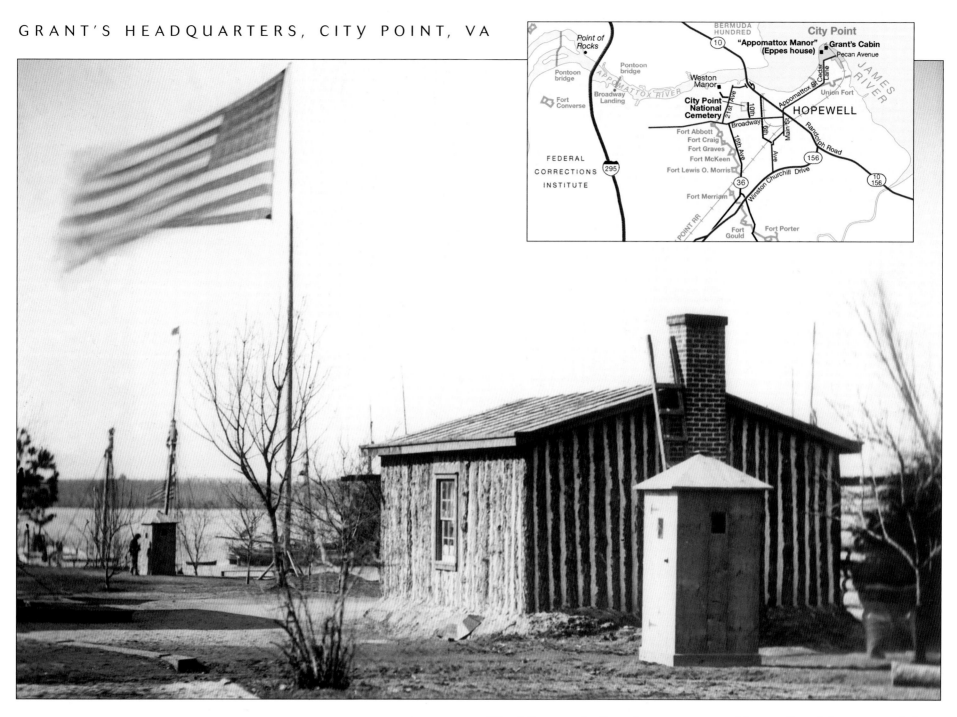

The failure to take Petersburg was a major blow to Grant's hopes to end the war in 1864. The fighting that raged just outside the city on June 15–18 held the promise of victory, but both the Union commanders and their troops were lacking the spirit and élan they displayed at the beginning of the campaign. Recognizing that his battered army was not in any condition to launch an attack against earthworks, Grant settled in for a siege.

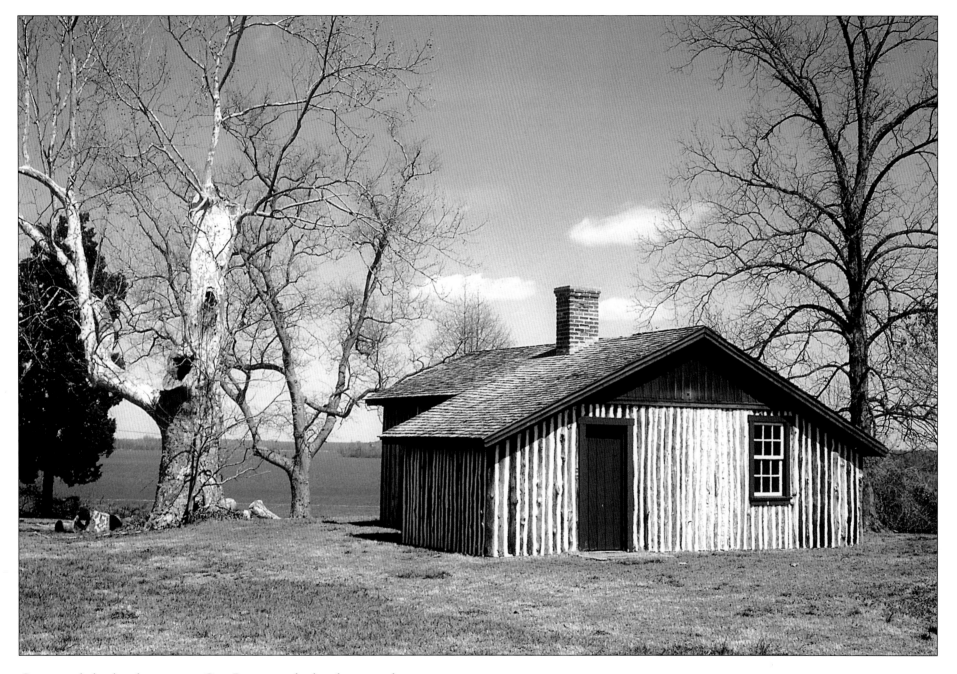

Grant made his headquarters at City Point, on the heights over the confluence of the James and Appomattox Rivers. Here, alongside Appomattox Manor, his aides and staff officers would build log huts and bivouac until April 1865. Of the multitude of huts, only Grant's would survive. After the war, it was taken to Philadelphia, where it rested for more than a century. Eventually, it was returned to City Point.

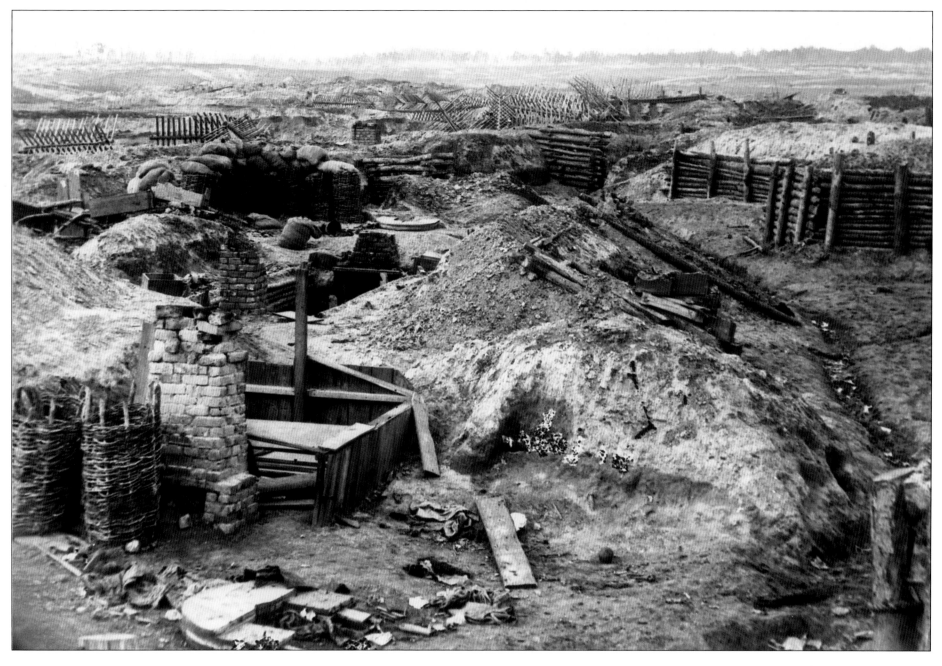

The brutal siege of Petersburg would consume nearly ten months and many lives. For America, the miles of dank and dirty ditches, connecting scores of equally dismal forts, were a precursor to the miserable trenches on the Western Front during World War I. At Fort Sedgwick, pictured here after the fall of Petersburg in April 1865, the fort's proximity to the Rebel lines made service in the bastion a particularly onerous ordeal.

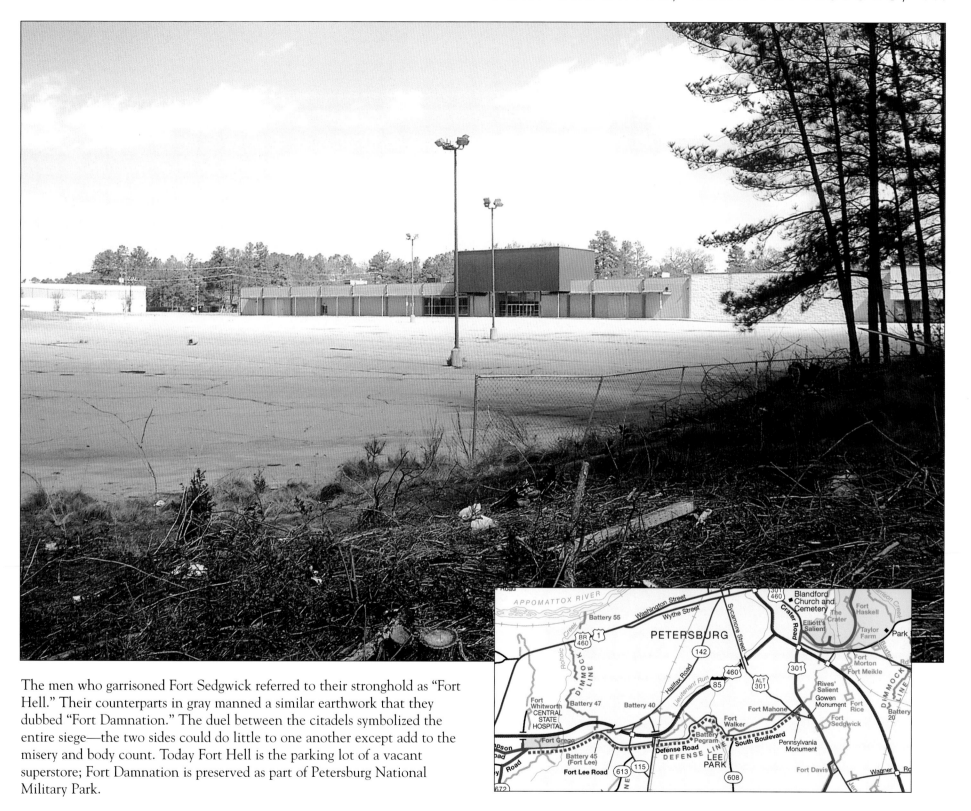

The men who garrisoned Fort Sedgwick referred to their stronghold as "Fort Hell." Their counterparts in gray manned a similar earthwork that they dubbed "Fort Damnation." The duel between the citadels symbolized the entire siege—the two sides could do little to one another except add to the misery and body count. Today Fort Hell is the parking lot of a vacant superstore; Fort Damnation is preserved as part of Petersburg National Military Park.

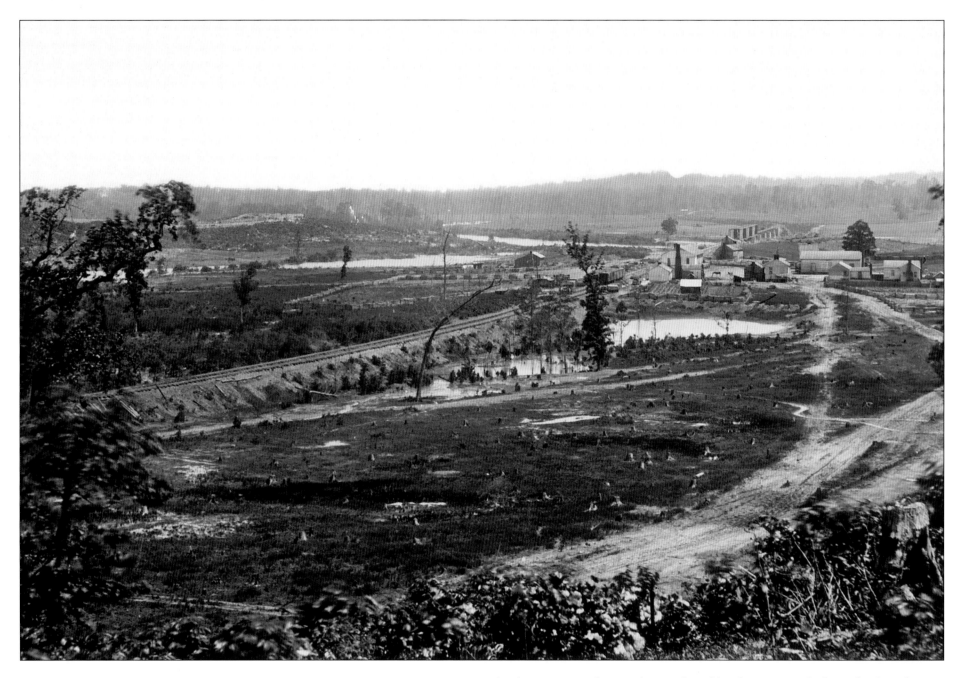

As the armies in the east began their bloody promenade from the Rapidan to Richmond, the principal antagonists in Georgia were engaged in a life-and-death struggle in northwestern Georgia. In early May 1864, Union General Sherman launched his spring campaign with Atlanta as its objective. After ten days of skirmishing and maneuvering, the armies wound up at Resaca, a strategic railroad town on the banks of the Oostanaula.

Sherman's goal had been to cut the supply line of his Confederate counterpart, General Joseph Johnston, by burning the railroad bridge visible in the wartime photograph. His first attempt, on May 9, 1864, failed because of an overcautious commander. His second try, on May 14–15, resulted in a stalemate, as neither side was able to land a knockout blow. On the evening of May 15, Johnston retreated across the Oostanaula, at the site of the present-day railroad bridge.

Sherman followed Johnston southward, nipping at his heels along the way. The two erstwhile adversaries fought a series of sharp but indecisive battles between the Oostanaula and Etowah Rivers. On June 27, 1864, Sherman abandoned his thus-far successful strategy of outflanking his opponent in favor of a frontal assault. Believing Johnston's Kennesaw Mountain line to be overextended, Sherman attacked the Confederates dug in along Pigeon Hill and Cheatham Hill.

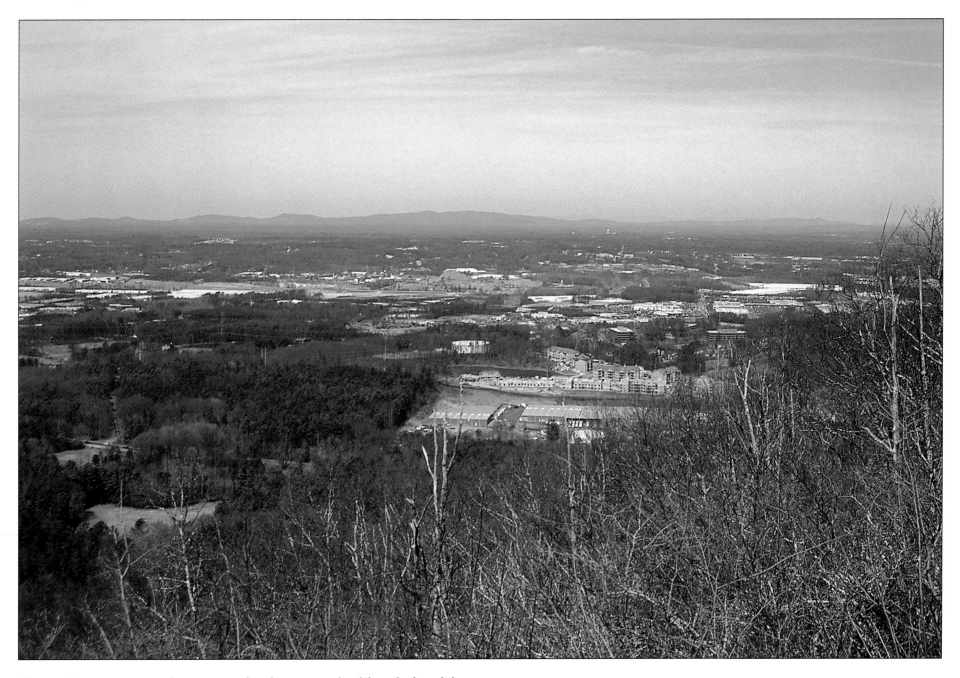

Sherman's men were simply not up to this daunting task, although they did manage to penetrate the Confederate line in several places. At Pigeon Hill in particular, the bluecoats secured the first line of Rebel trenches and seemed intent on exploiting their brief victory. The fight soon degenerated into a hand-to-hand brawl that would cost more than 4,000 lives. Today 2,884 acres of Kennesaw Mountain battlefield are protected from development.

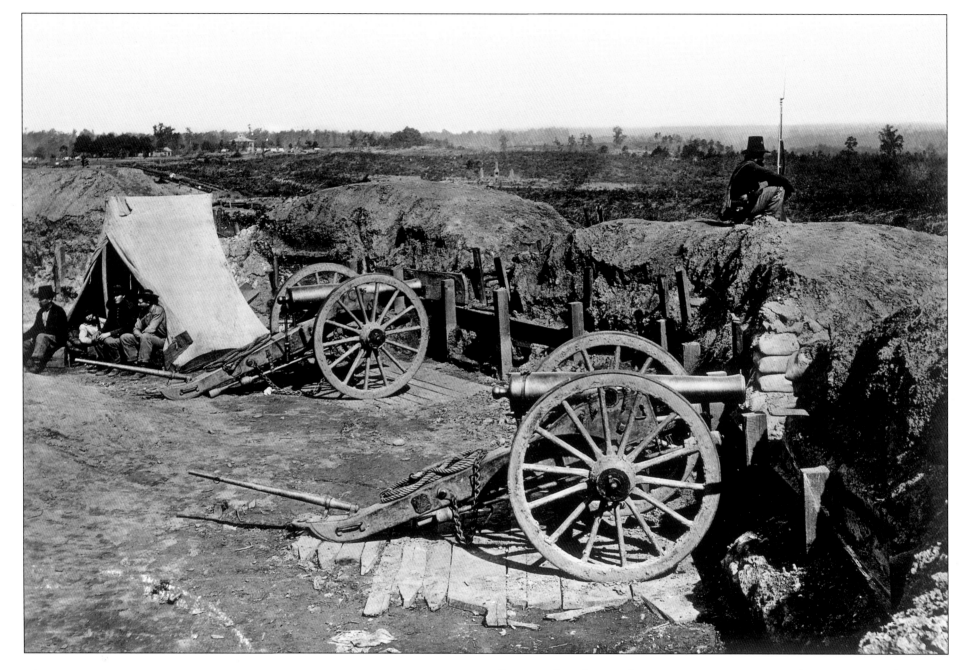

Smarting from his repulse at Kennesaw Mountain, Sherman returned to the flanking maneuvers that had proven so successful during the past seven weeks. Johnston was again forced to retreat, eventually falling back across the Chattahoochee River—the last water barrier between the Union forces and Atlanta. Johnston dug in, constructing a series of earthen forts around the city. However, the forts were destined to be defended by another man.

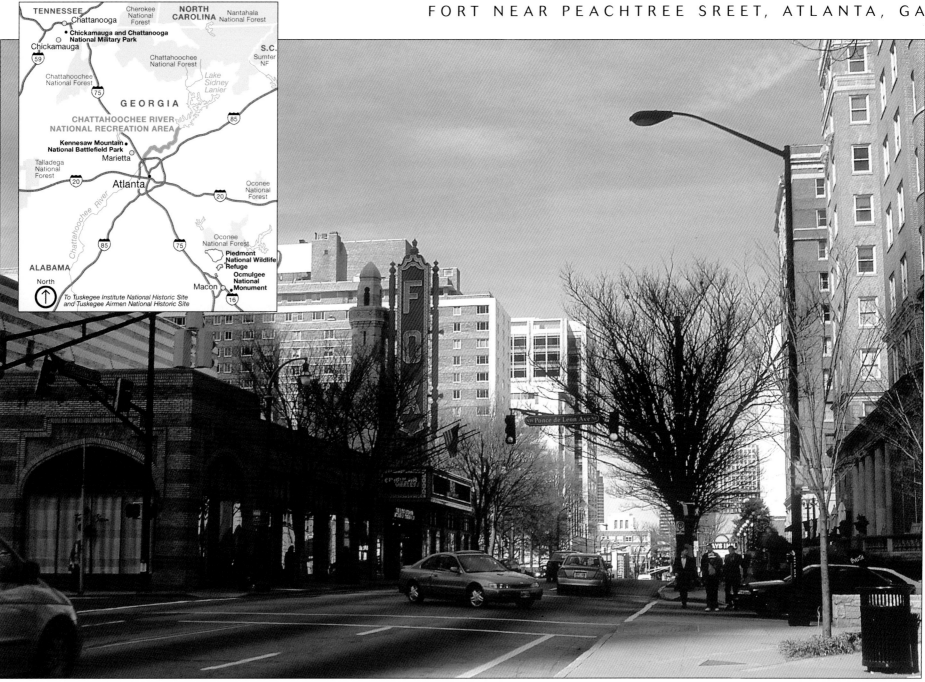

On July 17, 1864, President Davis replaced the cautious Johnston with General John B. Hood. Hood was not the type of commander who would wait to be outflanked by Sherman's host. He was determined to seize the initiative and throw the Unionists back from Atlanta. Three days after taking the helm, Hood sallied forth from his earthworks and threw his army against an isolated segment of the Federal army. Today residential housing sits where earthworks once stood.

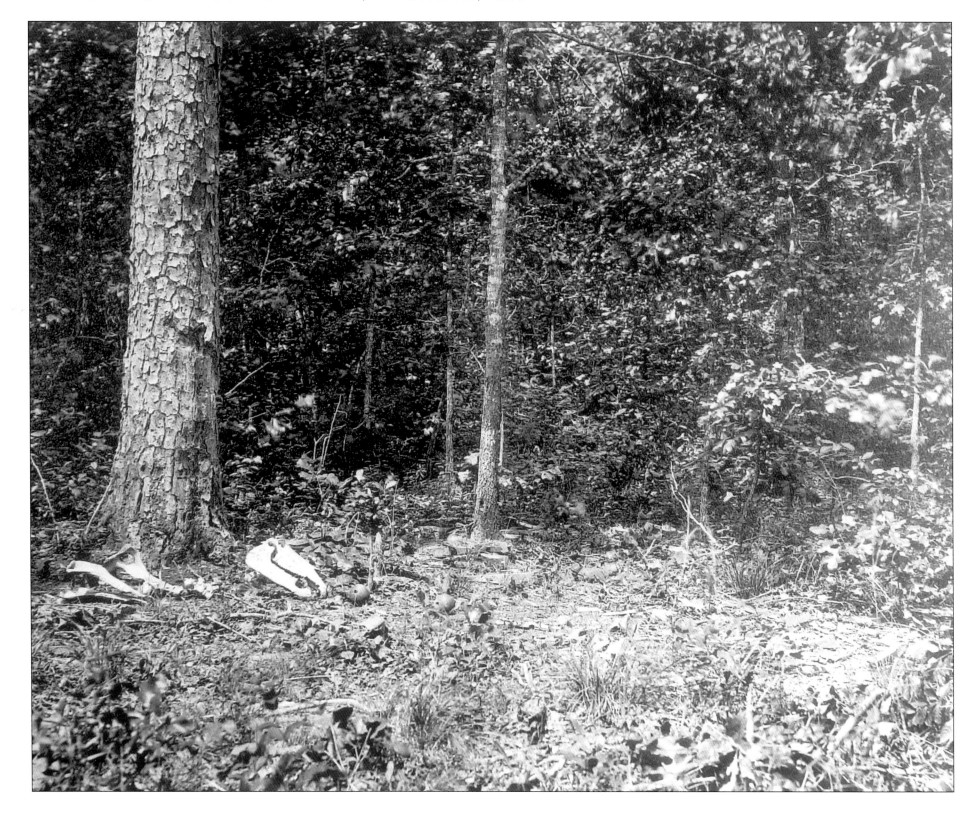

Left: The cost of the fighting around Atlanta was heavy on both sides. Hood's offensive at Peachtree Creek was followed by other, equally bloody battles that did little more than weaken the Confederate army's ability to hold its lines around Atlanta. One of the casualties of these early battles was General James McPherson, who was killed when he accidentally rode into Confederate lines. A Union photographer later captured the scene of McPherson's death.

Right: From the middle of July through the end of August 1864, Atlanta joined the long list of Southern cities besieged by invaders from the North. Hood's valiant but ill-fated attempts to reverse the Union tide only accelerated the inevitable. The fighting at Atlanta, Ezra Church, and Utoy Creek merely tightened Sherman's stranglehold on the city. Today a cannon marks the spot where McPherson was killed during the July 22 Battle of Atlanta.

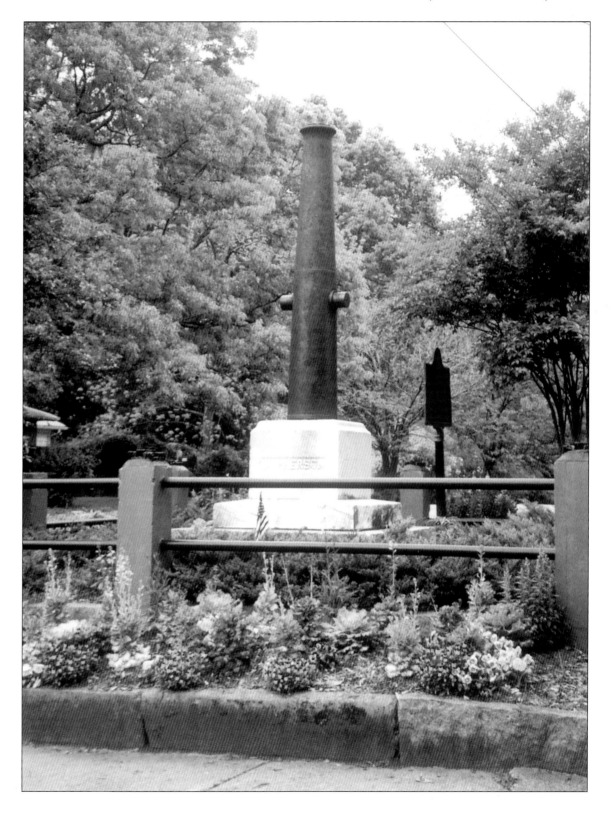

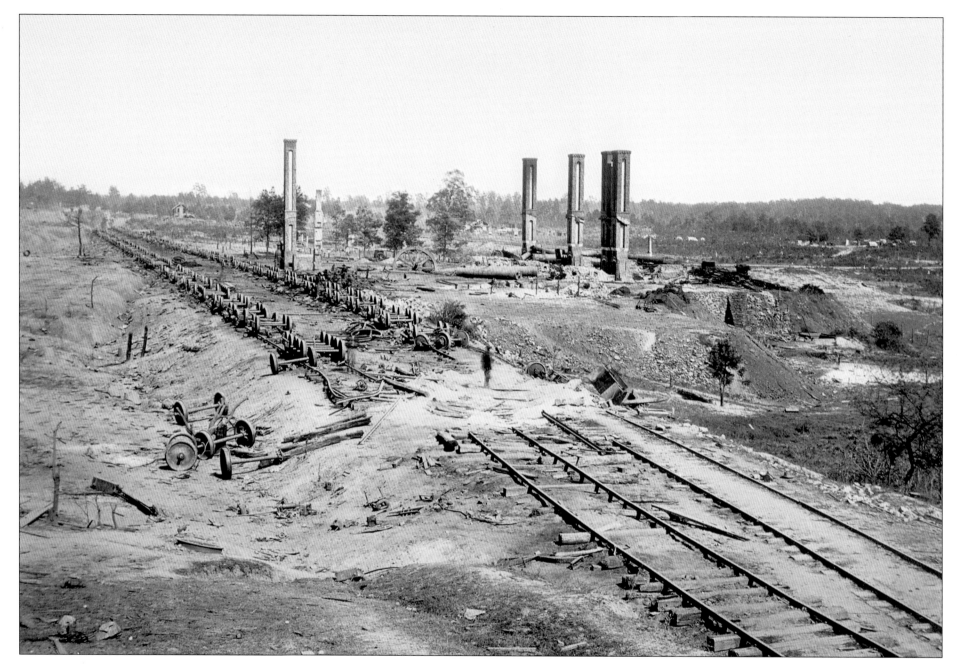

By the end of August 1864, an impasse had been reached. Hood's attacks had cost him more than 11,000 men, leaving his Army of Tennessee demoralized and dispirited. Meanwhile, Sherman was reluctant to attempt another flanking movement, fearing it would open his vulnerable supply line to attack. In the end, Sherman's excitability and impatience got the better of him, and on August 25 he launched an assault to take the city.

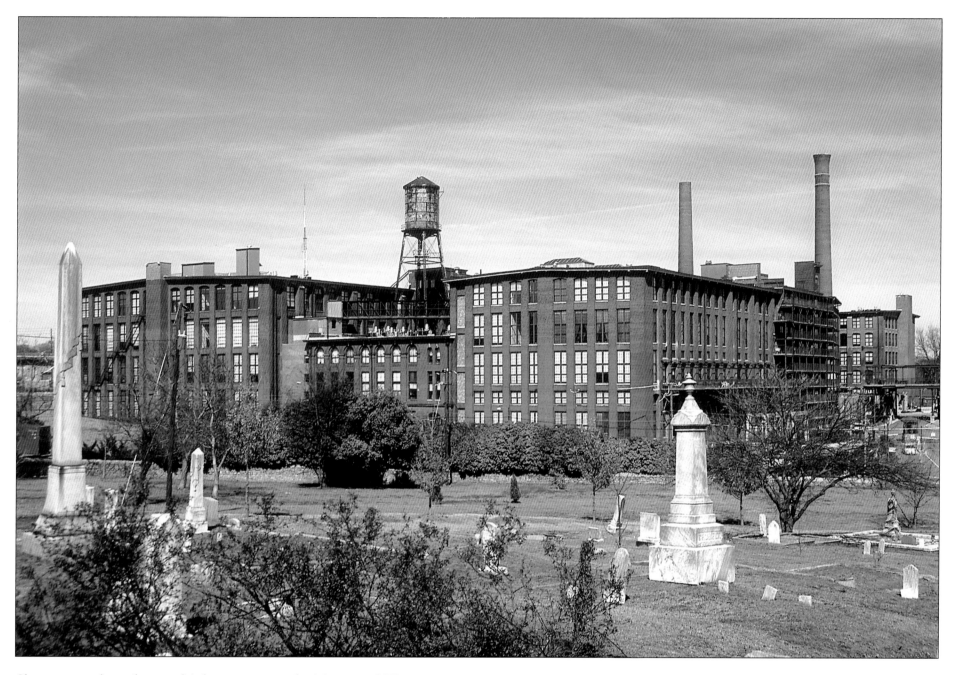

Sherman struck southwest of Atlanta, severing the Macon and Western Railroad, Hood's last remaining supply line. After a final, foiled attempt to regain the railroad at Jonesboro, Hood was forced to give up Atlanta. On the night of September 1, 1864, his battered army evacuated the city. When the triumphant Federals entered the city, they were witnesses to such scenes of devastation as the mill, shown in the period photograph, destroyed when a nearby ordnance train exploded. Today the location is unrecognizable.

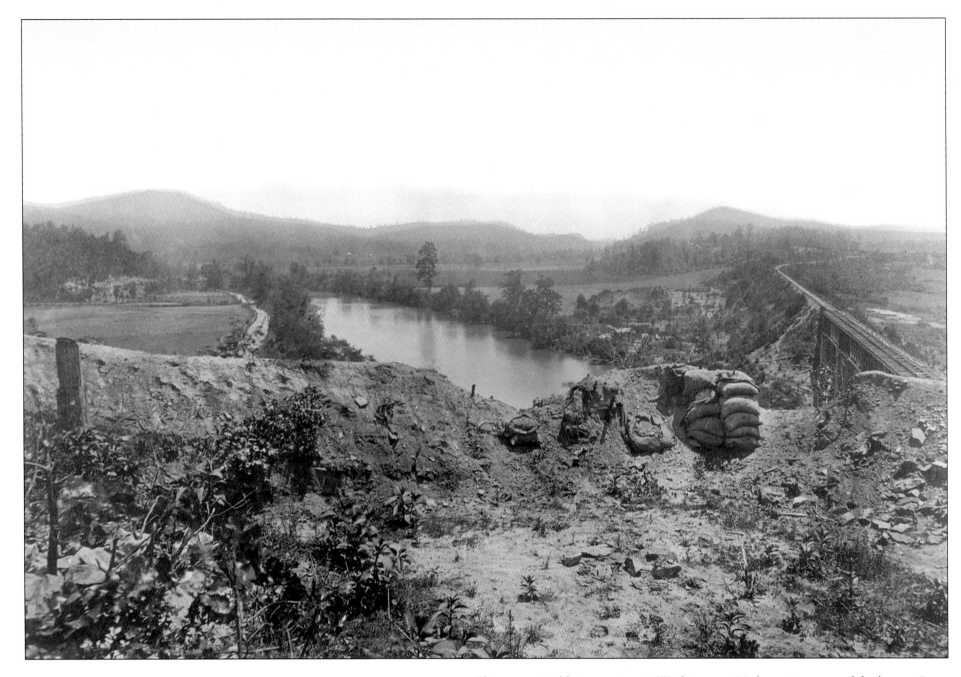

Sherman wired his superiors in Washington, "Atlanta is ours, and fairly won." Missing from the dispatch was any hint of where Sherman's army would march next. His victory left Sherman deep in hostile territory, dependent on a lengthy and vulnerable supply line that limited his options. Hood, sensing his opponent's quandary, began moving his army northward to strike the vital Western and Atlantic Railroad. On October 5, 1864, he struck the railroad at Allatoona Pass.

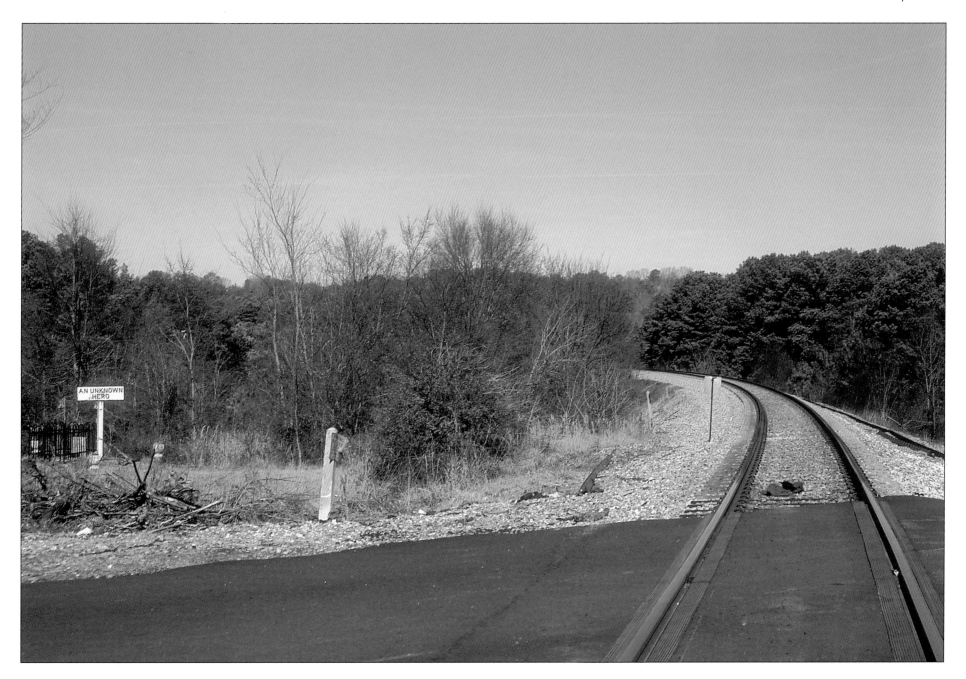

Unfortunately for Hood, Allatoona Pass was a natural citadel. The Union garrison, outnumbered by the attacking Rebels, prepared to make a final stand in the Star Fort overlooking the railroad. The stalwart Union defense of Allatoona Pass would inspire a postwar hymn entitled "Hold the Fort." Of the 5,300 men who fought at Allatoona, 1,600 became casualties—a combined loss of more than thirty percent. Today 272 acres of the Allatoona Pass battlefield are preserved as a park by the U.S. Army Corps of Engineers.

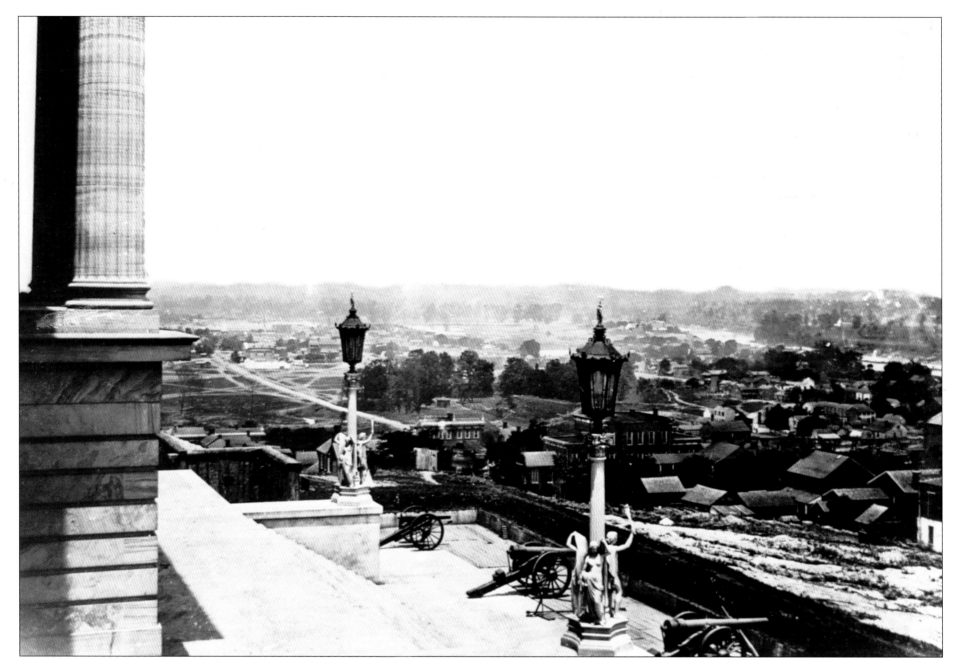

The bloody defeat at Franklin did little to dissuade Hood to march on Nashville. Although nearly a quarter of his army were casualties at Franklin, he pursued the Union army northward to the gates of the city, arriving on December 2, 1864. Fortunately for the Union cause, the methodical Thomas had been granted the time he needed to fortify the city, making it nearly impervious to assault. He even placed cannons on the steps of the state capitol building.

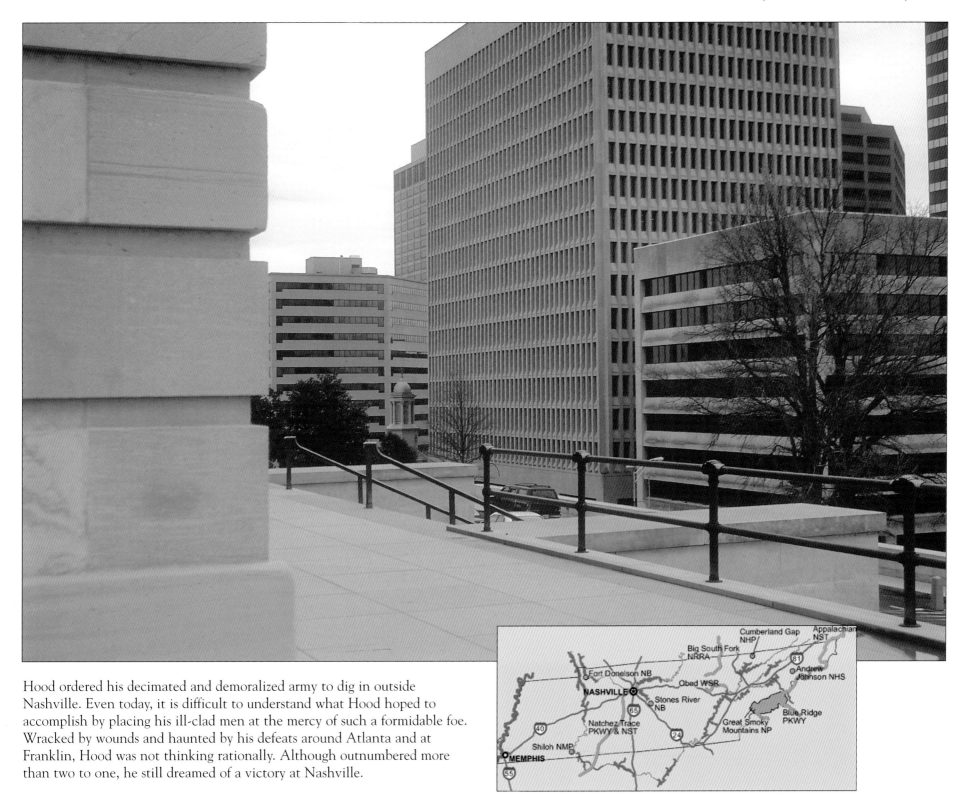

Hood ordered his decimated and demoralized army to dig in outside Nashville. Even today, it is difficult to understand what Hood hoped to accomplish by placing his ill-clad men at the mercy of such a formidable foe. Wracked by wounds and haunted by his defeats around Atlanta and at Franklin, Hood was not thinking rationally. Although outnumbered more than two to one, he still dreamed of a victory at Nashville.

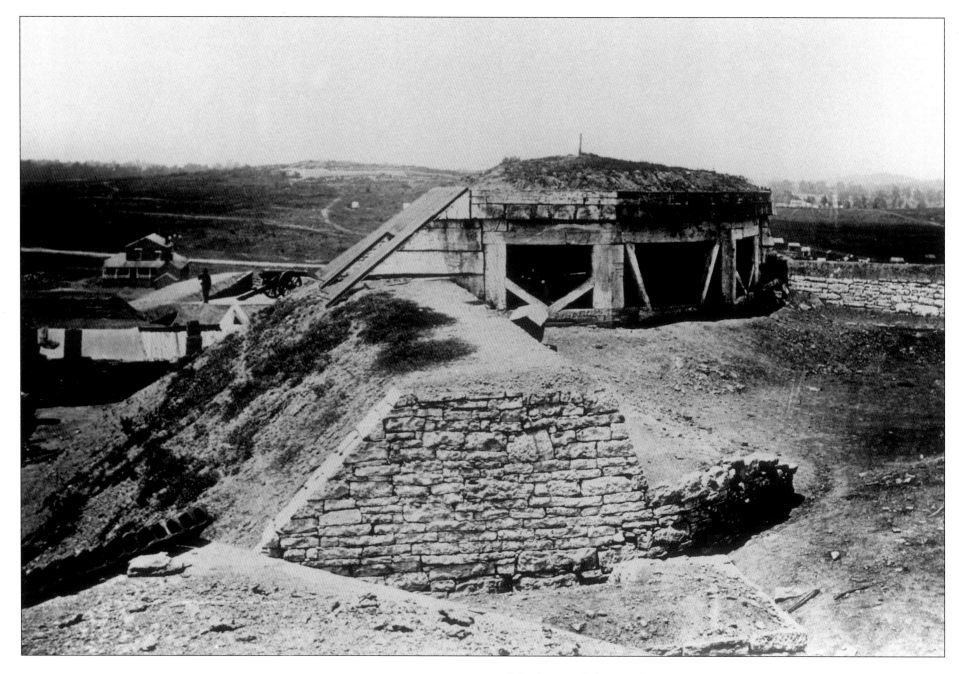

While the Confederates shivered in their lines outside Nashville, Thomas was slowly preparing to lift Hood's quasi-siege of the Tennessee capital. Too slowly, in the eyes of his overall commander, Ulysses Grant. Impatient with Thomas's sluggish performance, Grant was on the verge of replacing Thomas when the Army of the Cumberland finally ventured from its fortified lines. Shown here is the casemate of Fort Negley, one of the strongest points in the Union line.

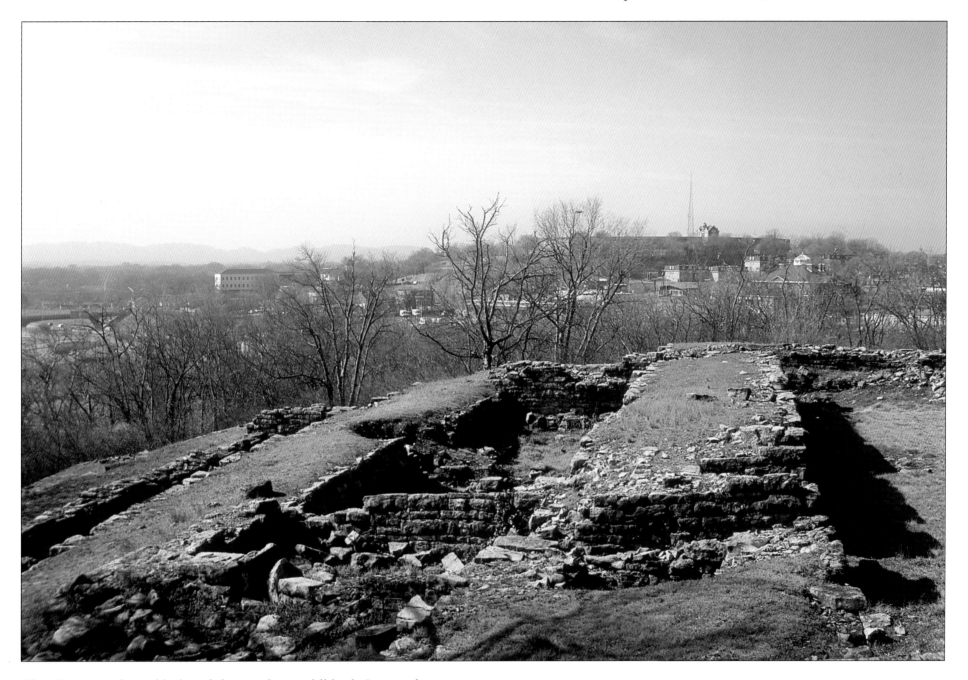

The Union attack quickly forced the gray line to fall back. Late in the afternoon of December 16, 1864, blue cavalrymen succeeded in infiltrating the Confederate rear, making the Southern line untenable. Attacked in flank and rear, the Rebel army collapsed, its shattered remnants streaming southward in disarray. Thomas's victory at Nashville crushed once and for all Confederate hopes for independence. Today, other than Fort Negley, little remains of this historic battlefield.

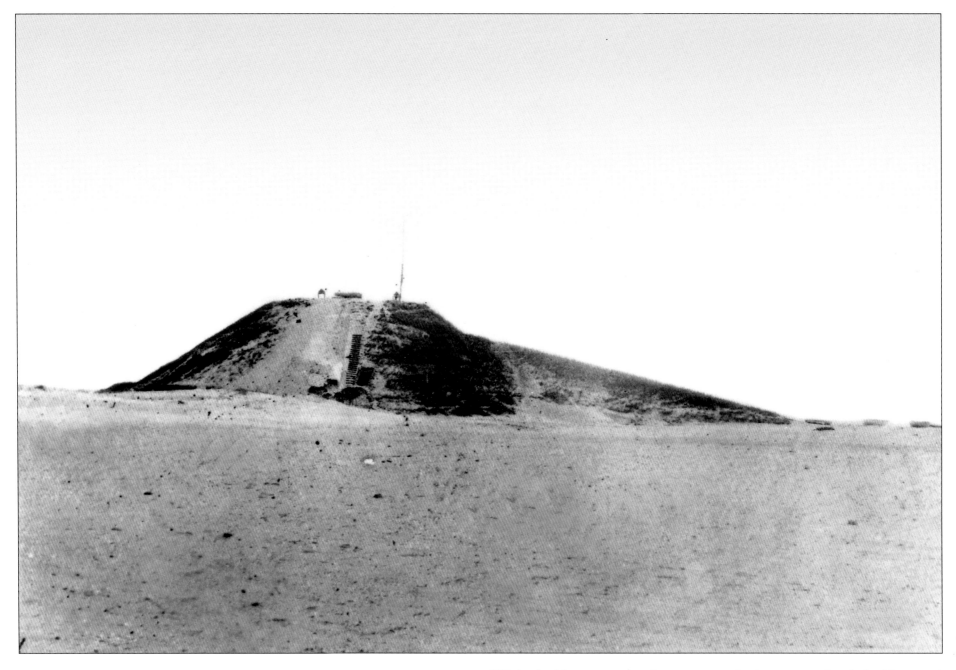

While the Union army was busy securing final victory on land, the Union navy was equally active winning the war at sea. The navy's target was the port of Wilmington, North Carolina—the South's only remaining outlet to the outside world. The port was guarded by Fort Fisher, an enormous earthen fortification armed with forty-seven heavy-caliber cannons. The fort was often referred to as the "Gibraltar of the Confederacy."

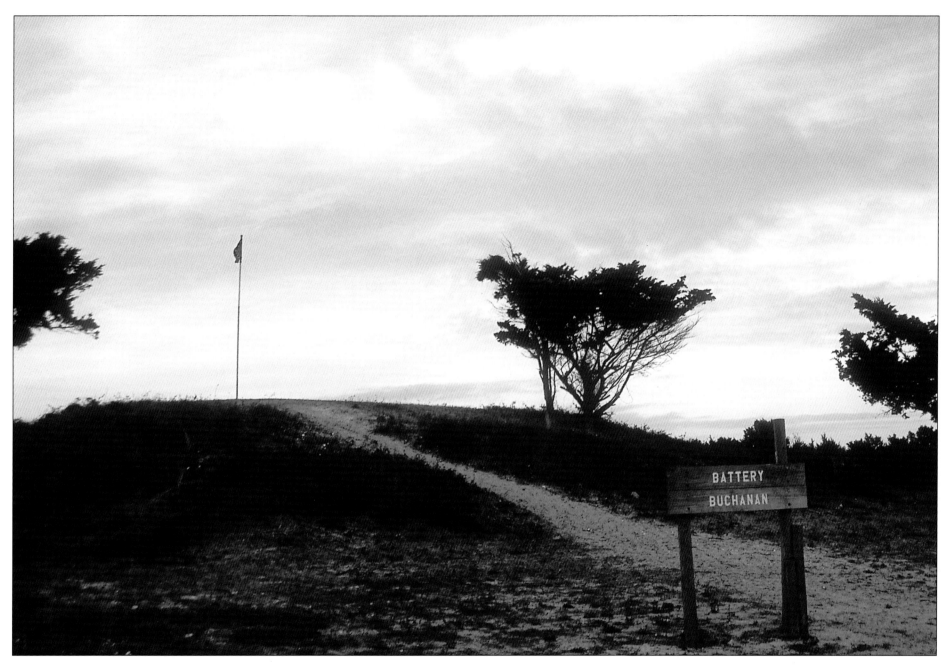

In December 1864, a joint army-navy expedition led by the absurdly incompetent General Ben Butler ended in embarrassment for the Union war effort. However, the Union troops regrouped and, under a new commander, launched a second attack in mid-January. After cutting the fort off from the mainland, Union forces launched two separate assaults and eventually breached the fort. After a hand-to-hand struggle, more than 2,000 Confederates surrendered. Today Fort Fisher is a state historic site.

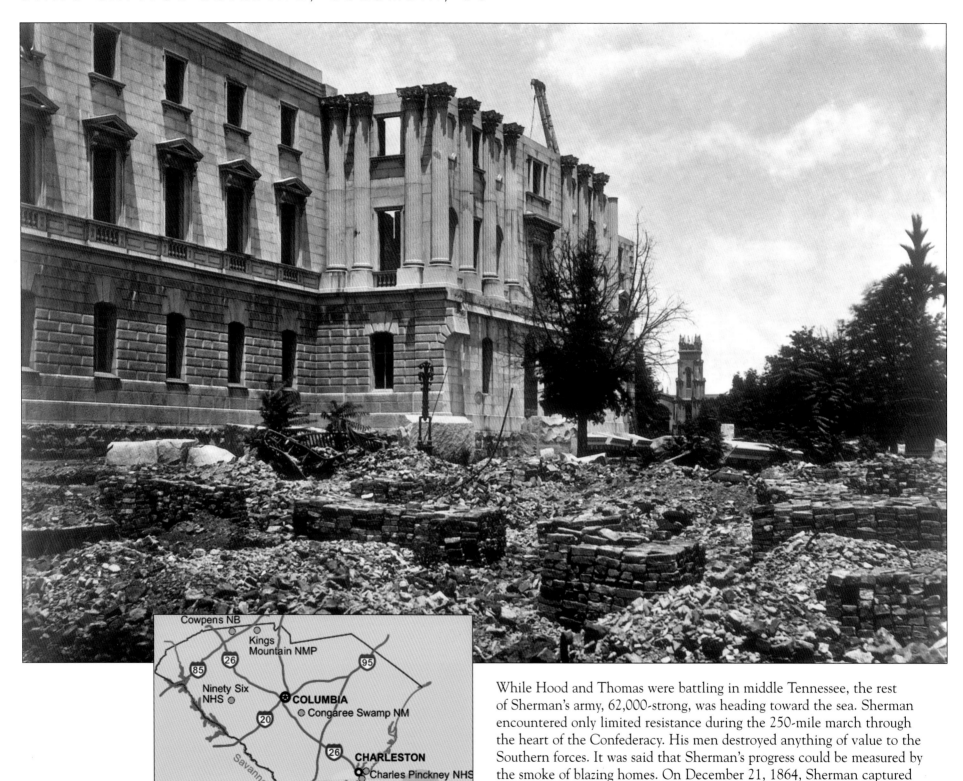

While Hood and Thomas were battling in middle Tennessee, the rest of Sherman's army, 62,000-strong, was heading toward the sea. Sherman encountered only limited resistance during the 250-mile march through the heart of the Confederacy. His men destroyed anything of value to the Southern forces. It was said that Sherman's progress could be measured by the smoke of blazing homes. On December 21, 1864, Sherman captured Savannah after an eleven-day siege.

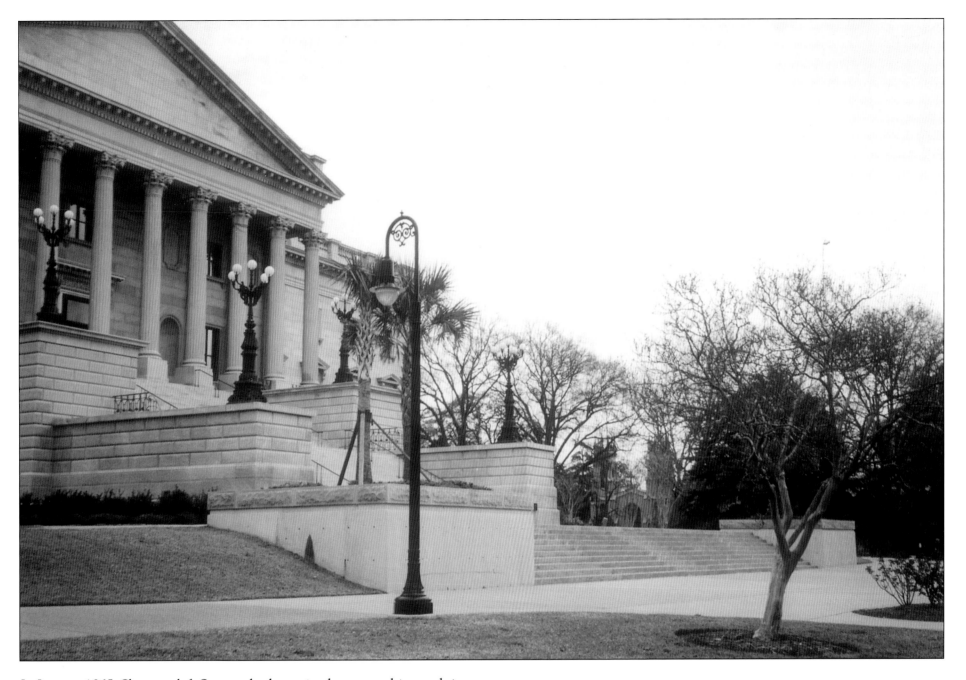

In January 1865, Sherman left Savannah, determined to repeat his march in the Carolinas. Although slowed by bad weather, Sherman's army could not be stopped. On February 17, his men marched into the South Carolina capital of Columbia. By the time they entered the city, part of the town was already ablaze with a fire that would destroy half its buildings. Among the structures gutted in the fire was the state capitol building. Today six bronze stars indicate where the building was hit by Union cannon fire.

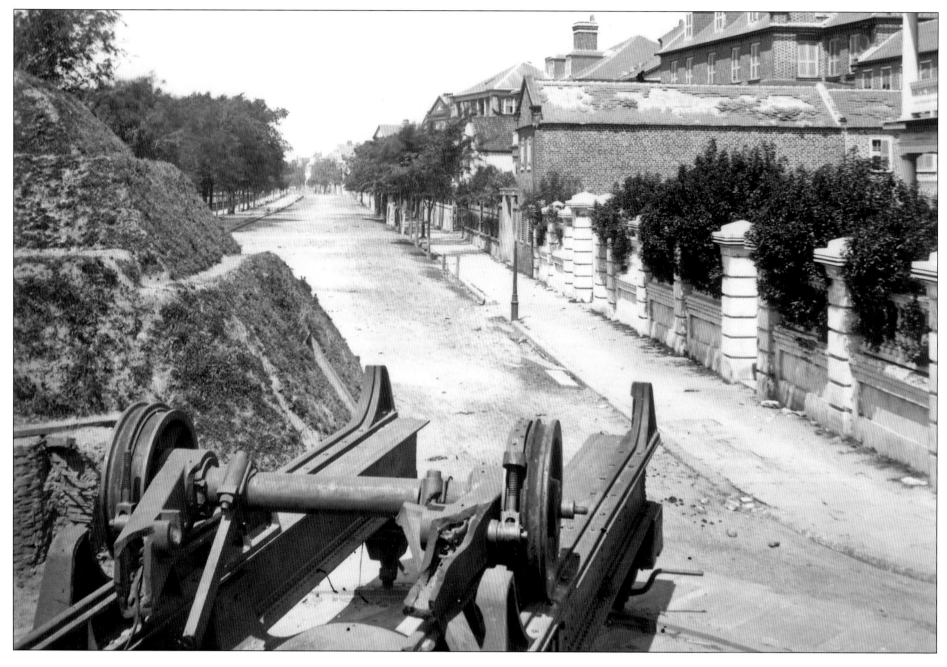

In addition to the capture of Columbia, Sherman's march through South Carolina resulted in cutting off communications with the port of Charleston. The Confederates had no alternative but to evacuate the city where the war began—a city that had come to symbolize Southern resistance. On February 17, 1865, the same day Columbia fell, the city was abandoned. Among the military ordnance destroyed was this enormous Blakely gun, imported from England.

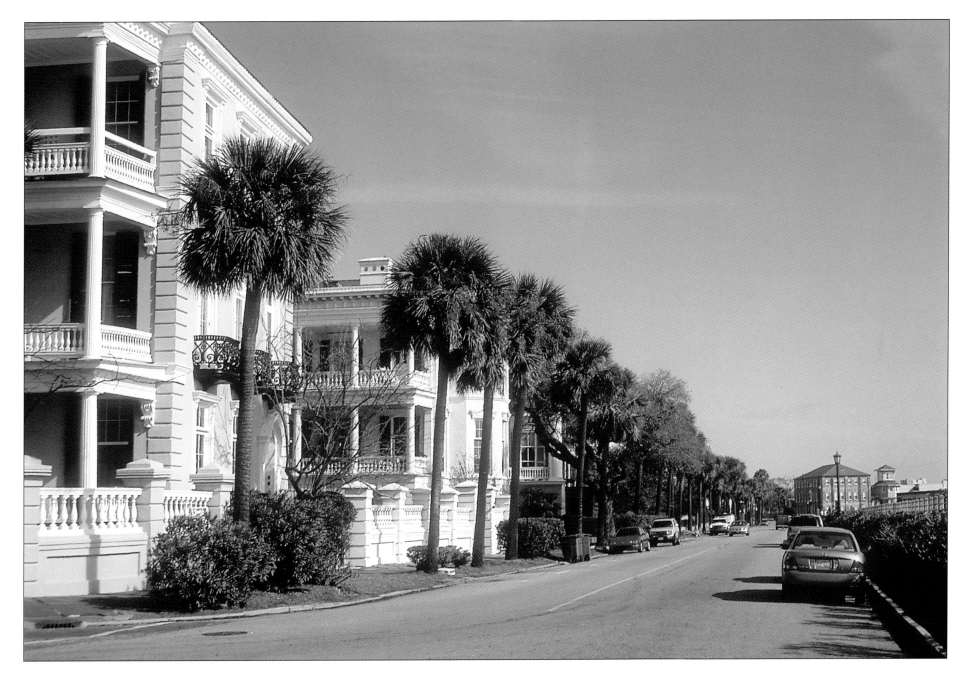

The fall of Charleston had an enormous effect on Southern morale. Confederate President Davis remarked that its fall to him was "extremely bitter." Conversely, the North was overjoyed with the capture of the city where secession began. On April 14, 1865, four years after the surrender of Fort Sumter, now-Union General Robert Anderson returned to Sumter to raise the flag he had been forced to lower in 1861.

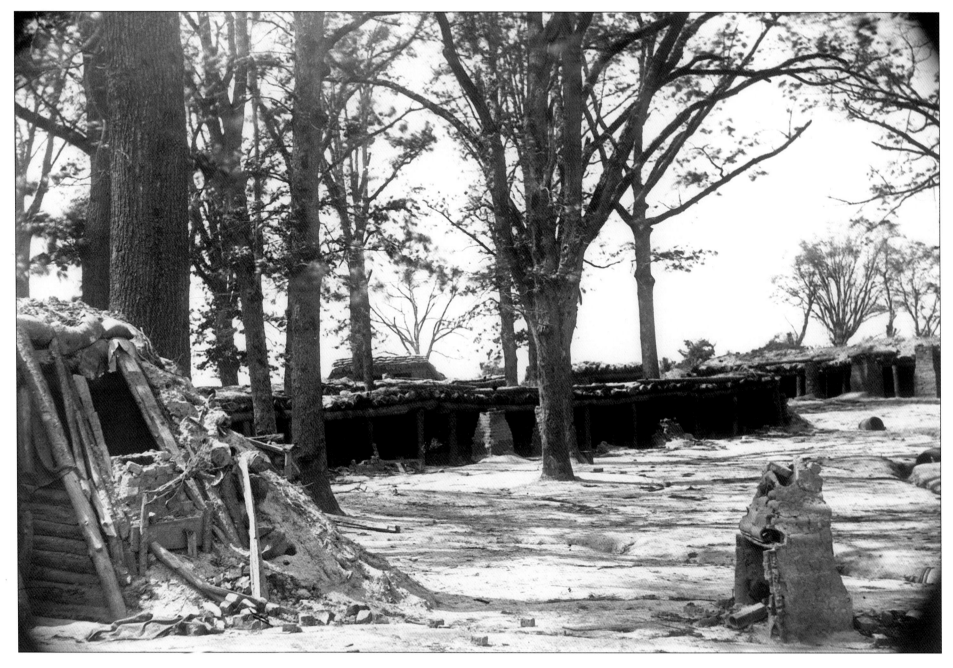

Back in Virginia, Confederate prospects were not much better. Although Lee still maintained his earthworks around Petersburg, his lines were being stretched to the limit. Only the muddy roads prevented Grant from launching an assault that would finally break the thin Rebel ranks. Seeing no other way out of his predicament, Lee decided to launch an assault against the Union host, hoping the attack would throw Grant off balance and allow his army to escape Petersburg unscathed.

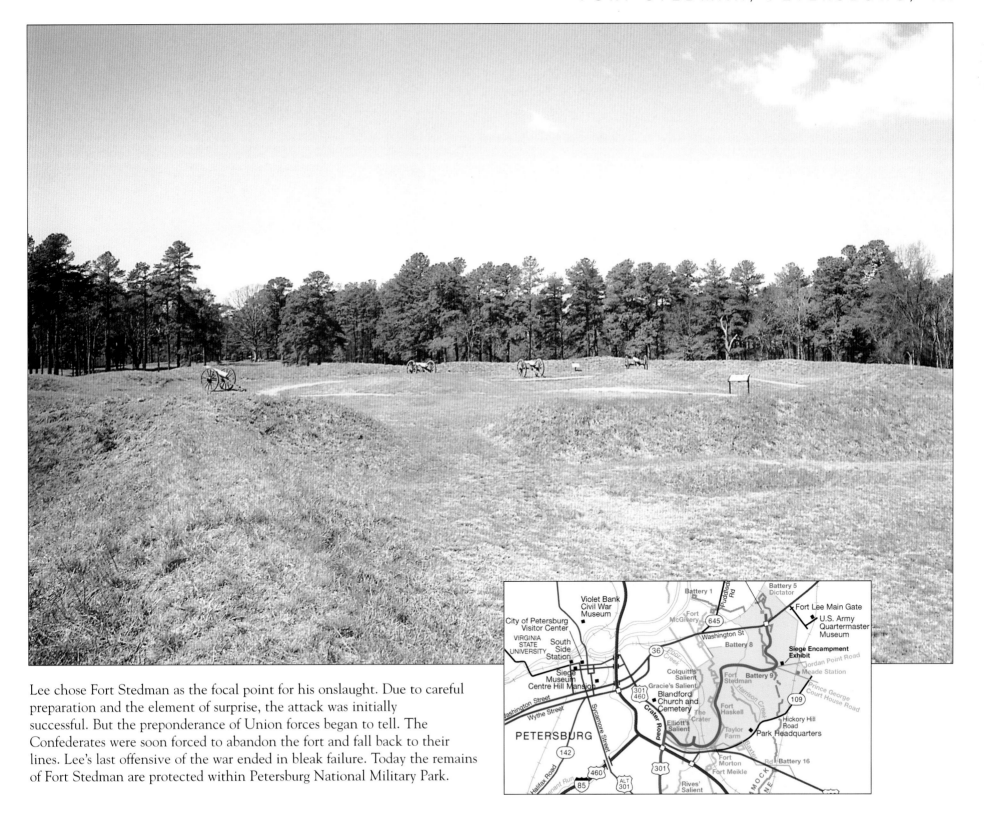

Lee chose Fort Stedman as the focal point for his onslaught. Due to careful preparation and the element of surprise, the attack was initially successful. But the preponderance of Union forces began to tell. The Confederates were soon forced to abandon the fort and fall back to their lines. Lee's last offensive of the war ended in bleak failure. Today the remains of Fort Stedman are protected within Petersburg National Military Park.

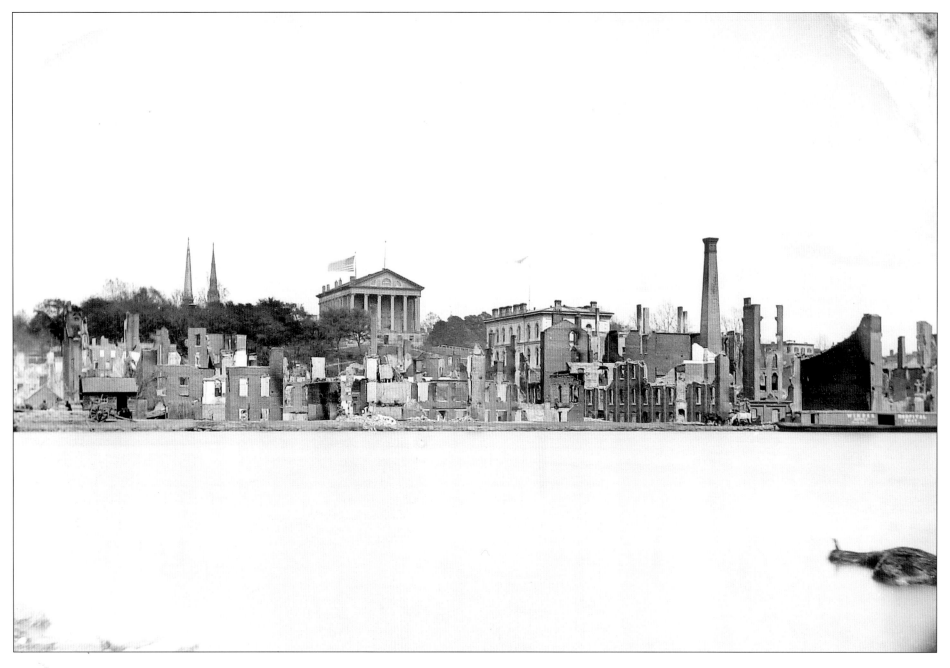

Within days of the repulse at Fort Stedman, Grant embarked on his much-anticipated offensive against Lee. On April 1, 1865, Grant crushed Lee's right flank at the battle of Five Forks. The next day, Grant moved in for the kill. His attacks on Petersburg forced Lee to evacuate the town, ending the longest siege in American history. Worse, without the vital rail junction of Petersburg, Richmond could no longer be held.

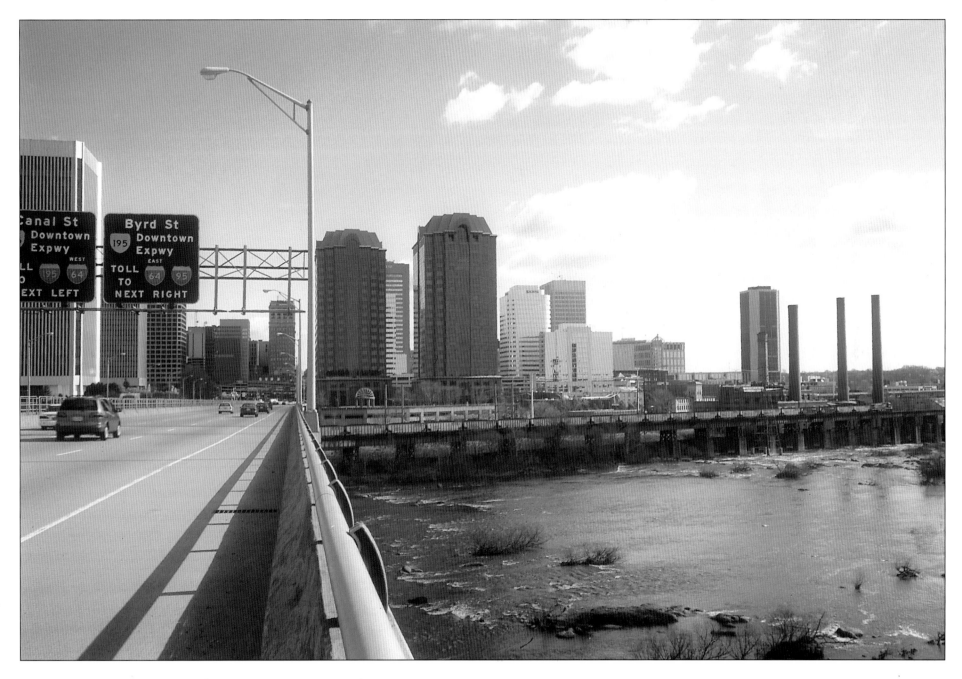

Throughout April 2, the Confederate government prepared to evacuate Richmond. That evening, President Davis, his cabinet and his army abandoned the city. Before leaving, the Southerners set afire anything that might be of value to the approaching Union army. The result was a conflagration that destroyed the warehouses and buildings along the riverfront. Today, the once-proud Confederate capitol is hidden from view behind a sea of modern high-rise office structures.

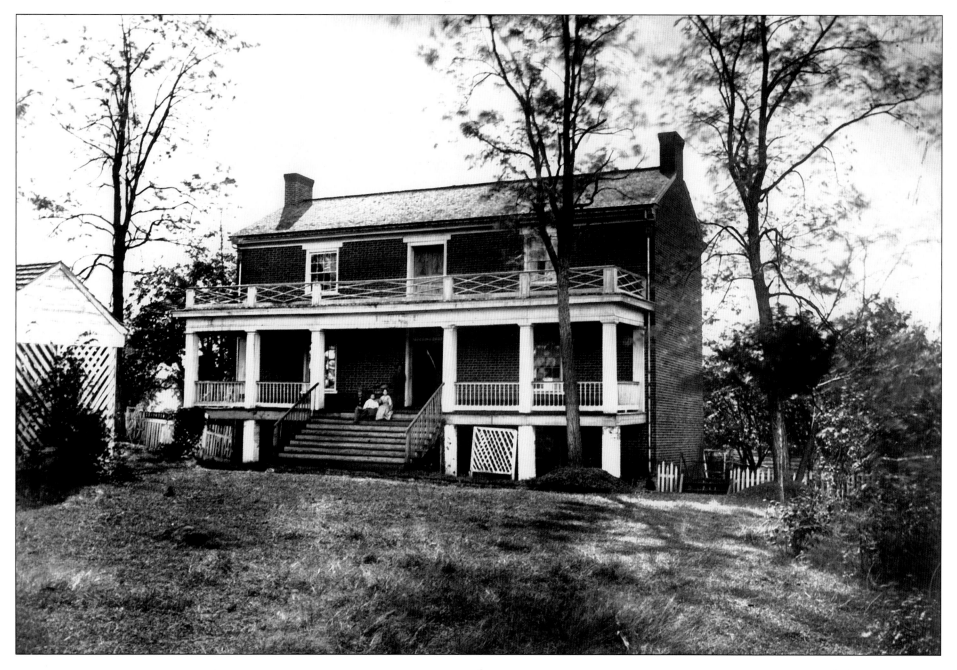

Freed from having to defend Richmond, General Lee hoped that his smaller, more agile army might still escape Grant's clutches to continue the war elsewhere. However, Lee's ill-fed, ill-clad men were no longer capable of the speedy marches that once dazzled the world. On April 9, the wily Lee was finally cornered at Appomattox Court House. That morning, he made arrangements to surrender his army to General Grant.

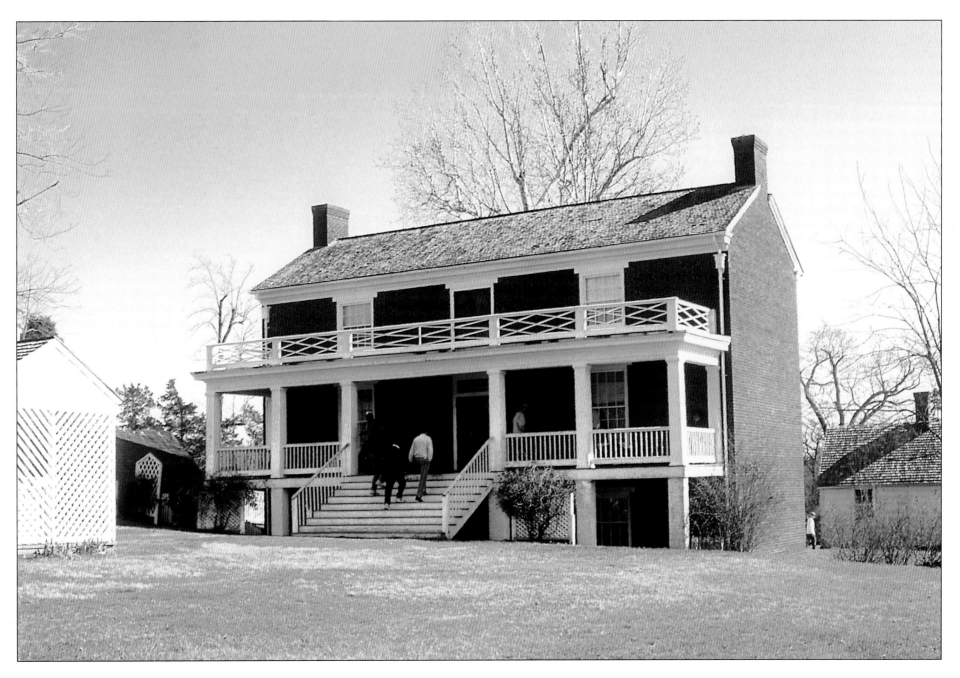

Grant and Lee met in the front parlor of the Wilmer McLean house, today preserved as a national memorial. There they exchanged small talk about their Mexican War experiences until Lee brought the conversation back to the capitulation of his army. Grant, famous for demanding unconditional surrender of his adversaries, offered generous surrender terms to Lee. Lee, moved by Grant's magnanimity, accepted the terms and surrendered his bedraggled but valiant army.

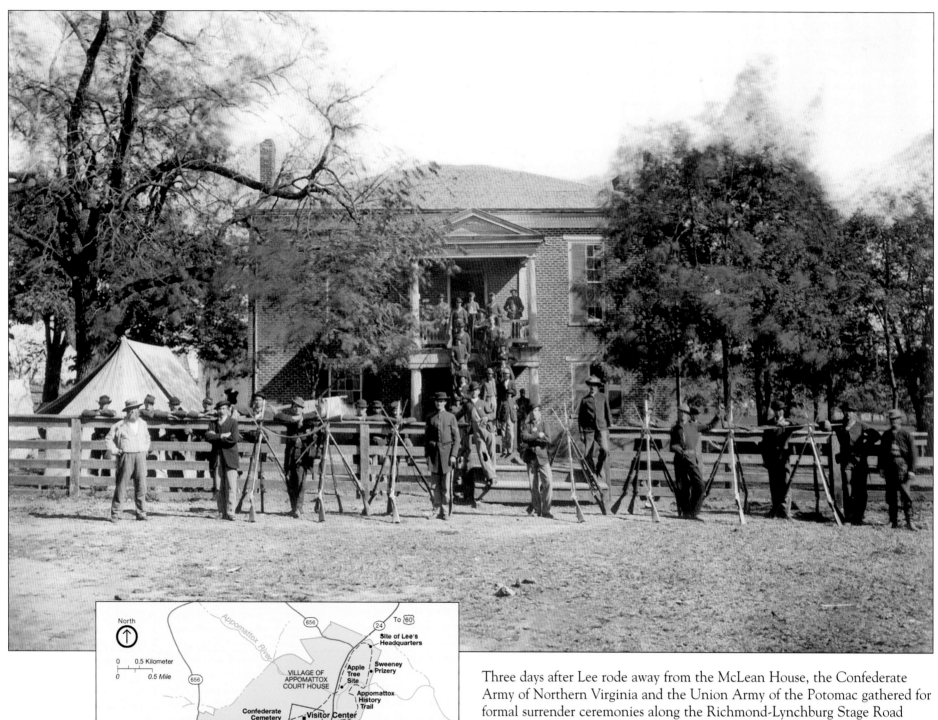

Three days after Lee rode away from the McLean House, the Confederate Army of Northern Virginia and the Union Army of the Potomac gathered for formal surrender ceremonies along the Richmond-Lynchburg Stage Road outside Appomattox Court House. The Southerners stacked their weapons, furled their tattered battle flags, and were free to go home. Following the surrender, several Union soldiers posed in front of the courthouse for photographer Timothy O'Sullivan.

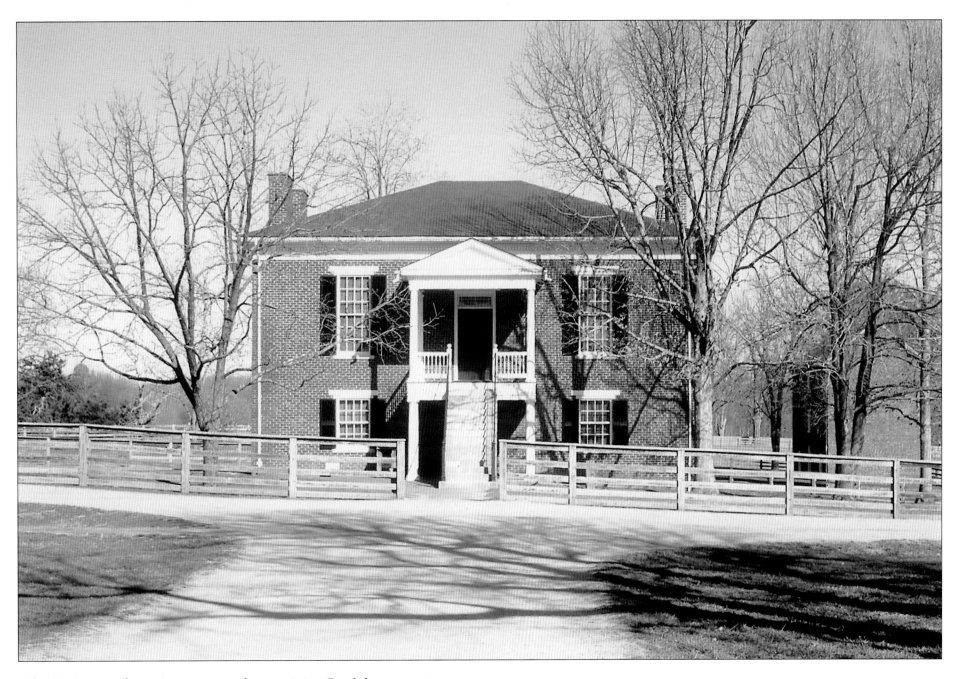

After Lee's surrender at Appomattox, the remaining Confederate armies
began to topple. Within a week, General Joseph Johnston, again in command
of the Southern army facing Sherman, approached his erstwhile adversary
about terms for surrender. By the end of May, nearly all the remaining
Confederate armies had capitulated. Today the former county court
house serves as a visitor center for Appomattox Court House National
Historical Park.

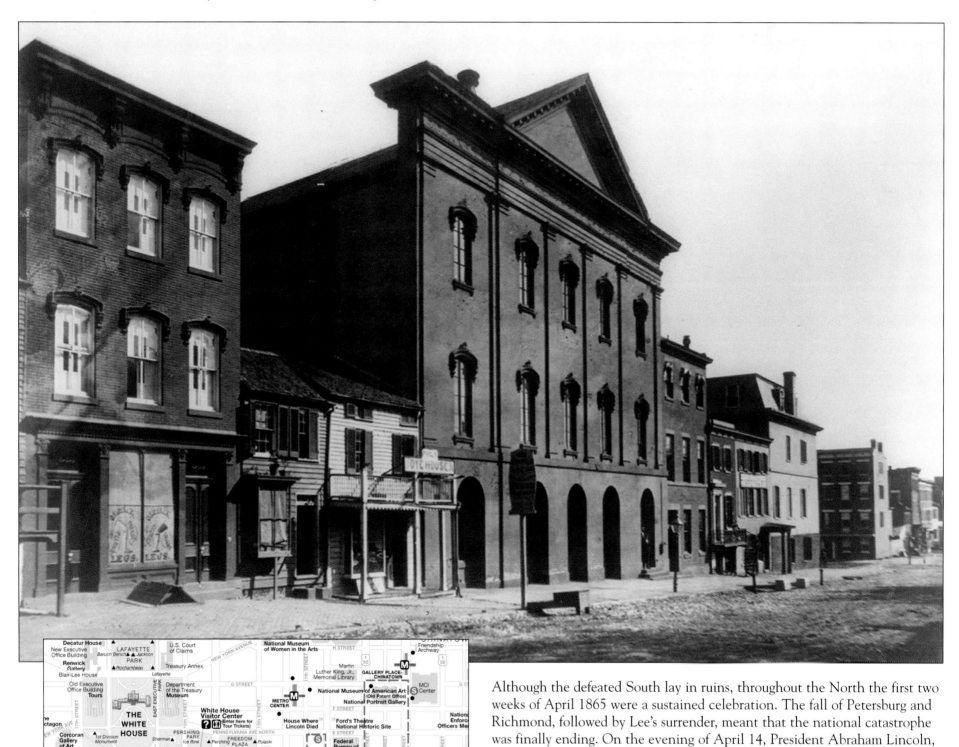

Although the defeated South lay in ruins, throughout the North the first two weeks of April 1865 were a sustained celebration. The fall of Petersburg and Richmond, followed by Lee's surrender, meant that the national catastrophe was finally ending. On the evening of April 14, President Abraham Lincoln, just beginning his second term in office, joined in the revelry by attending a play at Ford's Theatre featuring one of his favorite actresses, Laura Keene.

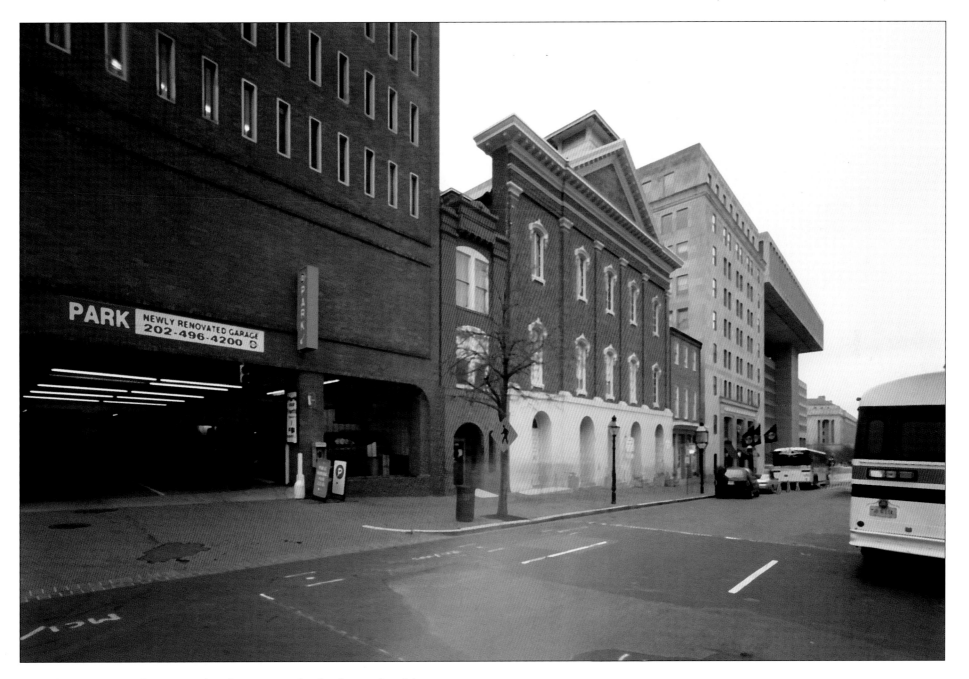

Lincoln's fatal wounding at Ford's Theatre was the final tragedy of the most tragic war in American history. Shot while sitting in the presidential box by actor John Wilkes Booth, the president succumbed to his wound in a small bedroom across the street from the theater. Upon his death, the Secretary of War was moved to remark, "Now he belongs to the ages." Ford's Theatre is now maintained by the National Park Service.

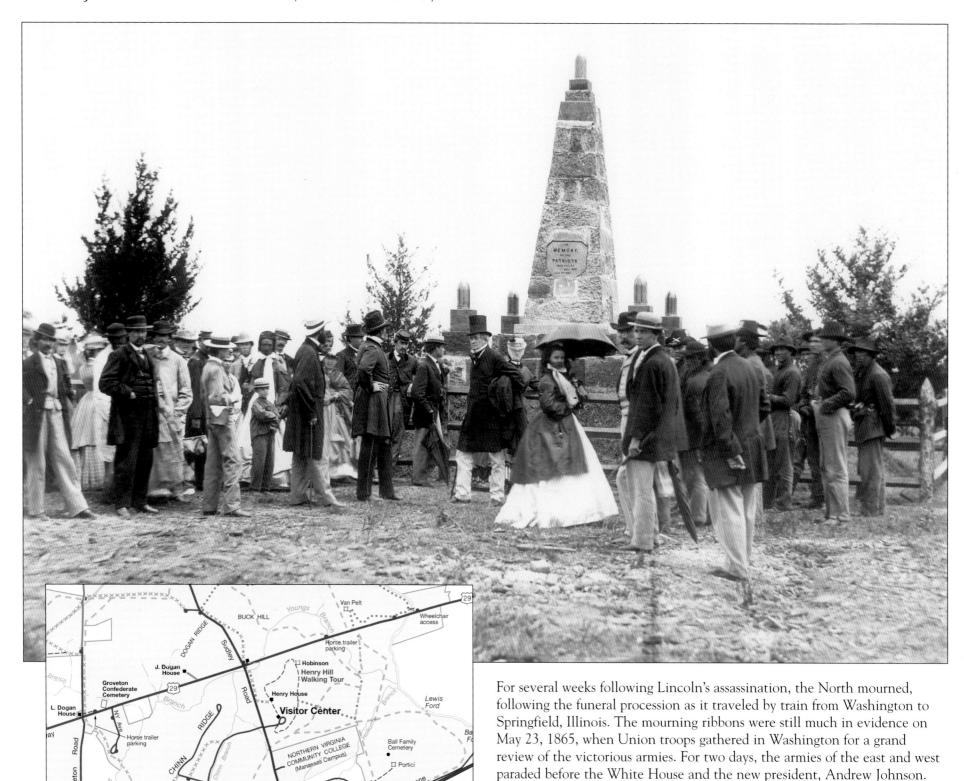

For several weeks following Lincoln's assassination, the North mourned, following the funeral procession as it traveled by train from Washington to Springfield, Illinois. The mourning ribbons were still much in evidence on May 23, 1865, when Union troops gathered in Washington for a grand review of the victorious armies. For two days, the armies of the east and west paraded before the White House and the new president, Andrew Johnson.

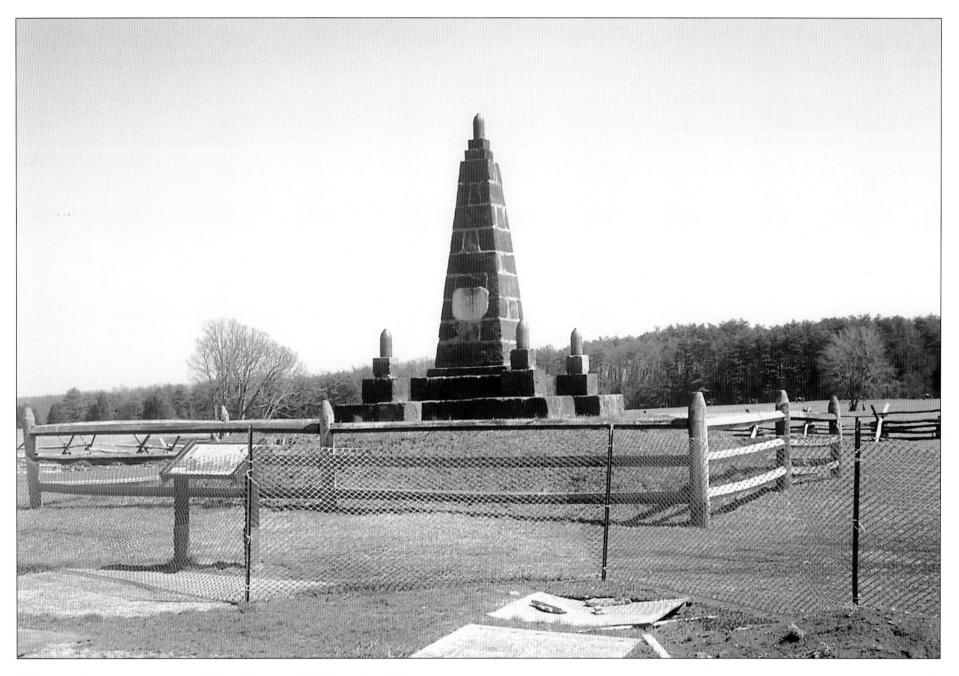

Following the review, veterans of the fighting at Bull Run decided to return to that haunting battlefield to commemorate their comrades who had died there. On June 10, 1865, two monuments were dedicated, one on Henry Hill and another near the deep cut at Groveton. Photographer Morris Smith captured the moment seen in the vintage photograph. Today both monuments are protected by the National Park Service; pictured here is the monument on Henry Hill.

INDEX